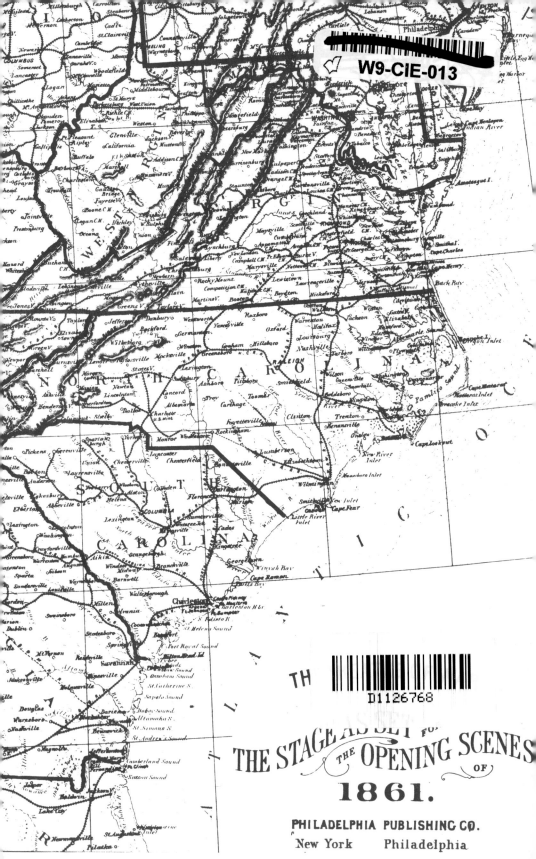

THE STAGE AS SET FOR THE OPENING SCENES OF 1861.

PHILADELPHIA PUBLISHING CO.

New York   Philadelphia

The Badge of Gallantry

THE BADGE
OF GALLANTRY

RECOLLECTIONS OF
CIVIL WAR CONGRESSIONAL
MEDAL OF HONOR WINNERS

Joseph B. Mitchell

White Mane Books
Division of White Mane Publishing Co., Inc.

First Printing, © 1968 by Joseph B. Mitchell, published by The Macmillan Company
Formerly Library of Congress Catalog Card Number: 68-25223

This White Mane Publishing Company, Inc. publication
was printed by

Beidel Printing House, Inc.
63 West Burd Street
Shippensburg, PA 17257 USA

In respect for the scholarship contained herein, the acid-free paper used in this book meets the guidelines for permanence and durability of the Committee on Production Guidelines for Book Longevity of the Council on Library Resources.

For a complete list of available publications please write

White Mane Publishing Company, Inc.
P.O. Box 152
Shippensburg, PA 17257 USA

Library of Congress Cataloging-in-Publication Data

Mitchell, Joseph B. (Joseph Brady), 1915-
    The badge of gallantry : recollections of Civil War Congressional
Medal of Honor winners / Joseph B. Mitchell.
        p.   cm.
    Originally published: New York : Macmillan, 1968.
    Includes extensive quotations from the Charles Kohen Collection of
letters originally requested by and written to James Otis Kaler.
    Includes index.
    ISBN 1-57249-093-4 (acid-free paper)
    1. United States--History--Civil War, 1861-1865--Personal
narratives. 2. Medal of Honor. 3. Soldiers--United States-
-Correspondence. I. Title.
E601.M69   1998
973.7'8--dc21   97-49155
                                                              CIP

PRINTED IN THE UNITED STATES OF AMERICA

Contents

FOREWORD   vii

INTRODUCTION: *Charlie Kohen and His Collection*   xi

I   FRATERNALLY YOURS   1

II   THE PASSING YEARS   15

III   INFANTRYMEN IN BATTLE   27

IV   BOOTS AND SADDLES   46

V   FORWARD THE GUNS   58

VI   ON SEAS AND RIVERS   71

VII   THE ANDREWS RAID   84

VIII   BOYS IN BATTLE   95

IX   THE VICKSBURG STORMING PARTY   111

X   GETTYSBURG   123

XI   NEGRO TROOPS AT CHAFFIN'S FARM   132

XII   OUR IMMIGRANT HEROES   144

XIII   BEHIND THE LINES   156

XIV   A BUGLE PEALED   172

INDEX   185

Foreword

THE idea of writing a book based upon a collection of over three hundred letters written by men who had won the Congressional Medal of Honor in the Civil War intrigued me from the very beginning. It seemed almost too good to be true that after all these years such a collection existed, and that the letters had never been published.

The first step was to make sure that they had not appeared in print before. In the late 1800's and early 1900's a number of books had been published describing the heroic deeds of individuals in the Civil War or the War Between the States. There was the massive *Congress Medal of Honor Legion*, weighing several pounds, written by St. Clair A. Mulholland, printed in 1905; the extensive two-volume work, *Deeds of Valor*, edited by W. F. Beyer and O. F. Keydel, published in 1903; and the series of books written by Medal of Honor winner Theophilus H. Rodenbough in the late 1800's.

If this book, *The Badge of Gallantry*, was to be new, featuring hitherto unpublished material, I would have to go through the slow, painstaking process of comparing each letter in the Kohen collection with all other material previously published. For, if an individual had been willing to tell one person of his experiences, he might have written the same story to others.

The three hundred letters were divided into two parts. One consisted of those letters written by individuals whose names did not appear in any other book, and there were a surprising number of these.

The remaining material contained letters from individuals whose stories had appeared in some of the other books. At first glance, I was afraid that most of these would also have to be excluded from consideration, although some were exceptionally good. Then, after careful comparison, letter by letter, I discovered that the authors or editors had apparently taken the material furnished them and rewritten the accounts, using only those portions of the basic letters that they wanted to see in print. As a result the most interesting parts were frequently deleted. Emphasis was placed primarily on the battle action only. Everyone was cast in a heroic mold. Criticisms and complaints usually disappeared. There was one exception to this general rule. It was a book entitled *The Story of American Heroism,* published by the Werner Company of Chicago and New York in 1896. This contained a number of the letters verbatim, so these could not be used. However, even in this book, some of the more humorous parts had been eliminated. At this point, I realized that the majority of the material in the Kohen collection was new and could be used, if properly presented.

The editing I have done on these letters has been of an entirely different nature. Some corrections have been made in spelling, punctuation, and sentence structure to make them more readable, but the thoughts, words, and ideas are those of the men themselves, as they expressed them.

After the text had been prepared, there came the problem of choosing appropriate illustrations. Charlie Kohen and I selected a few of the old photographs furnished by the individuals when they wrote their letters, but most of these old sepia prints had grown far too dim and faded over the years. I discussed this problem with Peter V. Ritner, Editor in Chief of The Macmillan Company. We agreed that I should search for wartime photographs, and for drawings depicting the battles in which these men had fought. If possible, the drawings should portray the specific actions described.

We wanted the work of artists who had been present, eyewitnesses such as Alfred R. Waud and Edwin Forbes. Furthermore we wanted to reproduce their original drawings if they had been preserved and were clear enough to be usable. If not, we could take the wood engravings made from their drawings and published in *Harper's Weekly* or *Frank Leslie's Illustrated Newspaper*. In this respect I was fortunate to have available to me, as curator, the facilities of the city of Alexandria's Fort Ward Museum, which has an unusually large collection of Civil War items, including a number of old books as well as copies of the magazines mentioned. But, of course, the greater part of the material came from the Library of Congress.

In a few special cases the paintings of artists done long after the war were chosen. An outstanding example of this was the painting of the Siege of Vicksburg done in 1888 by Thure de Thulstrup, whose rendition made one suspect that he had not only visited the battlefield but had also talked to the survivors of the Vicksburg storming party.

For the end papers I was particularly interested in trying to obtain a map that had been prepared during the years when these medal winners were writing their letters. In this respect I was fortunate to obtain through the Library of Congress a good one, not cluttered with military data, issued by the Philadelphia Publishing Company (copyrighted in 1893 by L. H. Everts), entitled "The Theatre of War, or The Stage As Set for the Opening Scenes, 1861."

This book took longer to produce than I had ever dreamed it would, and it would have taken longer still if it had not been for the aid given me by certain individuals. Chief among these was Charles F. Cooney. I am indebted to him in countless ways, far too numerous to describe here.

I wish also to express my gratitude to Robert S. Chamberlain and Lawrence B. Rivelli, who provided me with certain reference material that proved most helpful in my work.

For reading the chapter dealing with Negro Medal of Honor men, and offering constructive criticism for revision, I wish to thank Judge L. Howard Bennett, Director for Civil Rights in the Office of the Assistant Secretary of Defense for Manpower, and James C. Evans, Counselor for Civil Rights and Industrial Relations. They will find that in every case their suggestions and comments were incorporated.

I am also grateful to Wesley McPheron for his work of sorting the papers in the Kohen collection, the research he did, and for directing my attention to certain of the more interesting letters in that collection.

Robert Shosteck, curator of the B'nai B'rith Museum, the first president of the Jewish Historical Society of Greater Washington, and Sylvan M. Dubow, archivist of the Society, and a member of the staff of the Old Military Records Division, National Archives and Records Service, are both deserving of my special thanks for helping me in the research and the writing of that portion of this book dealing with Jews who were winners of the Congressional Medal of Honor.

The staff of the Prints and Photos Division of the Library of

Congress were of great assistance in my search for suitable material. They were most patient, cooperative, and helpful to me.

Finally I wish to thank Peter V. Ritner for his encouragement, sound editorial advice, and enthusiasm. Throughout the preparation of this book I knew that I could always count on him for help whenever a problem arose.

Introduction:

CHARLIE KOHEN AND HIS COLLECTION

CHARLIE KOHEN'S interest in the Civil War began a long time ago, many years before he acquired this unique collection of letters written by Civil War soldiers and sailors, describing how they had won the Congressional Medal of Honor.

In 1898, the year of the Spanish-American War, Charlie was a newspaper boy in Philadelphia. He soon discovered that many of his customers were veterans of that much greater conflict, the American Civil War. As is often the way with veterans, they were prone to indulge in stories. Charlie was a ready listener, and many of these old soldiers were his neighbors as well as his customers.

There was one former officer in particular who impressed him— Matthew S. Quay, who had been colonel of the 134th Pennsylvania Infantry. Late in 1862 Quay had contracted typhoid fever but, upon learning of the plans for the Battle of Fredericksburg, had refused to leave his command and had gone into battle with his regiment. The War Department citation for Quay's Medal of Honor reads: "Although out of service, he voluntarily resumed duty on the eve of battle and took a conspicuous part in the charge on the heights."

From time to time, the veterans would hold meetings at their homes. They let Charlie attend, so long as he promised to sit quietly and not interrupt. It was fascinating to an eleven-year-old to be permitted to listen to these men tell about the great conflict of over thirty years before.

But one thing puzzled Charlie very much. The country had just passed through another war, this time with a foreign power. Men from both North and South had fought together against Spain. There were four ex-soldiers on his paper route who lived near Charlie's home. Each of them had lost an arm or a leg in the war but they were never invited to the meetings. They were, of course, Confederate soldiers, but Charlie could not understand why, when a war had just been won by both North and South fighting together, these men could not also attend.

One evening, he stood up at one of the meetings, mentioned the four ex-soldiers and asked if they could come also. The chairman immediately wanted to know who had brought this boy and given him the right to speak. Explanations by Charlie's friends, neighbors, and customers were of no avail. A real hornet's nest had been stirred up; the meeting ended; Charlie was told that he was never to appear again.

Later he was forgiven and allowed to return, but his presence brought on another stormy argument. At a third meeting, Matthew Quay spoke in favor of having the Confederate soldiers attend, reminding his audience that we were all Americans, and that it was time to forget past differences. Even his influence failed to sway those opposed until a special meeting was held in City Hall. There it was finally agreed that the ex-Confederates could come and take part in the discussions, but not be permitted to vote.

This was Charlie Kohen's first experience with a veterans' organization. Perhaps the problems he encountered may have served him in good stead in the years to come when he would be confronted with much greater obstacles in trying to help the veterans of other wars yet to be fought.

When World War I began, Kohen was working in New York City. He remembers enlisting on the steps of the New York Public Library and choosing the cavalry as his branch of service. Eventually, however, he was assigned to the 7th Division and served in combat with it in France. In 1919, Charlie returned to Philadelphia, then moved to Washington, D.C., where he opened a shop on Pennsylvania Avenue near the Capitol, selling stamps, coins, and manuscripts. Shortly afterward, he joined the Vincent B. Costello Post No. 15 of the American Legion and became interested in helping the wounded and disabled men in Walter Reed, Mt. Alto, and the Naval Hospital in Washington. To say that he became active in this work would be an enormous understatement. It would be more accurate to say that he dedicated his life to the task. For a person like

Charlie Kohen veterans' problems presented a tremendous challenge. It became a gigantic task, often keeping him busy from nine o'clock in the morning until midnight.

In the years immediately following World War I there were no governmental agencies capable of providing adequately for veterans' needs. Nor were there any private or volunteer organizations that could deal with such problems. As a result, numerous ex-soldiers and sailors were being discharged from hospitals, perhaps in the dead of winter, with inadequate clothing, thin suits, worn and shabby shoes, and no overcoats. Charlie soon discovered this fact and began making the rounds of the department stores in Washington, persuading their owners to donate what they could to aid these men. Many of the stores, large and small, contributed generously. When the American Legion discovered what Kohen was doing, they made him chairman of their permanent Welfare Committee. Later, the Veterans of Foreign Wars appointed him to serve in the same capacity. It is almost impossible to determine how many items of clothing were distributed in this way. A newspaper article, written in 1928, credits him with being responsible for distributing over 4,600 overcoats, nearly 6,000 suits of clothes, and over 7,000 pairs of shoes to needy veterans. Socks, ties, and shirts were not counted. Furthermore, when discharged, these veterans, who came from every part of the country, often had no money. With the assistance of the Travelers' Aid Society, half-fare railroad tickets were furnished so that they could reach home.

One wonders that his business survived, especially when he began to expand his activities to provide amusements and shows in the hospitals. Charlie made the rounds of all the leading theaters in Washington to obtain their support. He remembers Roland Robbins, the manager of Keith's Theatre, asking him the same question that President Calvin Coolidge asked: "Charlie, how much is the American Legion paying you for all this?" His answer was the same to both: "Not one cent." Mr. Robbins then explained that he had not meant to hurt Charlie's feelings, adding: "It will be to your advantage when show people know about it."

Some of the greatest names in show business consented to appear in Charlie's shows, including McIntyre and Heath, Eddie Cantor, and Jimmy Durante. Charlie, who was usually the master of ceremonies, discovered on one occasion that Oscar Hammerstein had slipped into the audience. With Broadway and 42nd Street now on his side Kohen's Hospital Productions were well on their way. Over the years, a total of more than 1,000 professional shows were given to hospital patients and at local army camps.

Although he neglected his business, Kohen's name became known and this in turn brought many prominent people to his store. One of his coin customers was Henry Ford, who wrote a letter from Dearborn, Michigan, noting an error of ten dollars in a bill submitted for coins purchased, although the letter does not say in whose favor the error had been made.

In 1925, Charlie was elected commander of the Vincent B. Costello Post of the American Legion. Some years later he became commander of Columbia Post No. 833 of the Veterans of Foreign Wars. It should not be surprising to learn that during these years Charlie received a number of citations and awards. He was the first recipient of the Watson B. Miller Award for outstanding service to the District of Columbia American Legion. The D.C. Veterans of Foreign Wars gave him the Citation of Merit. Hundreds of letters came from the Red Cross and from the hospitals where he worked so diligently. He particularly treasures two letters he received when he staged a special benefit performance at Walter Reed Hospital for a veteran who had lost his eyesight in World War I. The letters came from General John J. Pershing and Mrs. Woodrow Wilson.

It was through his efforts that, for the first time in history, in a veterans' hospital, radios with earphones were installed for the patients at the Naval Hospital in Washington, D.C. Charlie arranged this with the help of the well-known "Roxy" of New York City, and through the generosity of Julius Rosenwald, president of Sears Roebuck, who refused to permit his name to be mentioned as donor. This service was then extended to other hospitals in the area.

Charlie will never approve of this account of his activities if the names of four people who helped him in providing for the veterans are not included. They are: Colonel Julius I. Peyser, also a member of the Costello Post; George H. Maines, one of the founders of the American Legion; Joseph F. Barr of the American Legion and the Jewish War Veterans; and Stilson Hutchins, founder of the Washington *Post*.

On July 3, 1930, Charlie was married to Sallie Cohen of Washington, D.C. Shortly thereafter they moved his shop, this time to Seventeenth Street, which, incidentally, put it close to the White House and an avid stamp collector named Franklin D. Roosevelt, whom Charlie saw often at his place, now operating as the Hobby Shop.

When the Jewish War Veterans were organized in Washington, D.C., Kohen promptly joined Post #58 and continued his work, representing all three veterans' organizations. He arranged an annual automobile outing for veterans, was prominent in the American Legion's yearly boys' "Soap Box Derby," and played an important role in the development and promotion of junior baseball in Washington, D.C.

In 1938, Stephen Kaler appeared at the Hobby Shop with a huge box of letters written by Civil War winners of the Congressional Medal of Honor. He explained that these letters had been obtained personally by his father with the intention of writing a book, which he published in 1896 entitled *The Story of American Heroism*. Because of his great interest in the Civil War, Charlie gladly bought the letters. Then a week later his visitor returned with another large box, full of more letters. It took Charlie three months just to look over the papers to see what he had acquired. He discovered that the letters had all been written in the 1890's by soldiers and sailors who had fought in the Civil War. The letters were addressed to a Mr. James Otis, who had asked these men to describe in their own words how they had won the Congressional Medal of Honor. Obviously this huge collection could not simply be handed to a publisher. Someone would have to sort the letters, make selections, add explanations as needed, and them put them together in a logical sequence and in an attractive form. Charlie knew that he could never do the work himself. He was neither a writer nor a historian. Yet he felt that these letters should be published as originally promised the Medal of Honor men who had written them.

Before he could find someone to undertake this tremendous task World War II intervened. Charlie found himself handling the American Legion Bond Drive in Washington, and also serving on the Selective Service Board that covered the White House area and registered President Franklin D. Roosevelt. This duty lasted for over

twenty years; Charlie later became the chairman of the White House area board and is the recipient of a special certificate in honor of his long service in this capacity.

Thus, for several more years the existence of these letters written by Civil War Medal of Honor winners remained a secret. The pressure of events kept F. D. R. from visiting the Hobby Shop during the last years of his life, but Harry S. Truman came frequently. After he became President the shop was again moved, this time to its final location in Georgetown, on Wisconsin Avenue.

President Truman's principal interest, Charlie recalls, was in old coins, but the friendship developed during those years has not diminished. When Truman heard through his former military aide, Major General Harry H. Vaughan, that this book on Medal of Honor winners was being written he sent word to Charlie that if there was any way he could assist, he would be happy to do so.

The first news account telling of the existence of these letters appeared in *The New York Times* in November 1952. Paul Kennedy had persuaded Charlie to let him write a story about them. One month later another article appeared in the Baltimore *Evening Sun*. Again permission had been granted; the author of this story was William Manchester. With so much interest aroused in his collection, Kohen talked to his friend John Justin Smith of the Chicago *Daily News* about writing a book based on the letters. Smith felt he could not, in view of his other commitments, undertake such a time-consuming task but, to further the project, he also wrote an interesting news article telling about the collection. Then Major General U. S. Grant, III, chairman of the Civil War Centennial Commission, sent a letter to the Hobby Shop urging publication.

However, the next time the Kohen name appeared in the press it was in connection with an entirely different subject. On October 20, 1962, on his seventy-fifth birthday, Charlie presented to the Library of Congress a collection of 9,000 Calvin Coolidge letters, without charge to the government—not even declaring the gift a tax deduction. Two years later Drew Pearson, in a column entitled, "What they did for their country," drew attention to this unusual donation, and also told his readers that Kohen had arranged for two other unique gifts to the Smithsonian Institution. These were the first Henry rifle presented to President Lincoln for the use of the

Union Army in the Civil War, and the first airplane flown by Orville Wright, which was acquired through the efforts of Henry Ford.

The next step in the chain of events leading toward publication of the Kohen collection came through a visit to the Pentagon. There Charlie met Wesley McPheron, who worked for over a year, doing research, sorting papers, and working on various letters that he felt should eventually be used in the book.

The entire project was then presented to the author. Another year and a half had to pass before the text could be presented to the publisher. General Grant had been right when he told Charlie: "It is later than you think, when you consider the time it will take to put them in order and in condition for publication."

Editor's Note:

The vocabulary of race that Colonel Mitchell used in the preparation of this book was that appropriate to his times. The editor chose not to change his words in this reprint in order to preserve the integrity of this classic work.

The Badge of Gallantry

" 'I am not conscious of having done more than my duty. . . . There were scores of gallant men of my regiment who served with me who are just as much entitled to the medal as I am . . .' "—*Wartime photo of John Wainwright*

I

Fraternally Yours

"I AM not conscious of having done more than my duty in any of the many engagements in which I participated with my regiment during its four years of service. I always aimed to do my level best and to do that as promptly as possible. I have noticed that the quicker such work as charging an enemy's fortifications is done, when once the charge is on, the better it is for all concerned.

"I was a first lieutenant, but in command of my regiment, in the assault on Fort Fisher, North Carolina on 15 January, 1865, and had been in command for several months previously. At the very outset of the attack, while rapidly forming my regiment for the charge on the works, I was severely wounded in the right shoulder. Notwithstanding this I continued in the fight from first to last, about seven hours, having secured a lodgement in the northwest angle of the fort. With a few others of my regiment, I advanced from traverse to traverse until we secured an advanced position on the parapet of the fort which we held until the final surrender of the works, having been in very close contact with the enemy during the whole time, and in several hand to hand encounters with them.

"I received the personal thanks of General A. H. Terry, commander of the expedition, for services in the battle. He invited me to his quarters the next day for that purpose.

"There were scores of gallant men of my regiment who served with me who are just as much entitled to the medal as I am, and thousands of soldiers everywhere in the war do deserve it. A little temporary prominence brought me to the attention of my superior officers at the assault on Fort Fisher."

This letter was written from Wilmington, Delaware, in the early 1890's by John Wainwright in response to a request that he give his personal story of how, some twenty-five years before, he had won the Congressional Medal of Honor.

A man who signed himself as James Otis, and gave his return

" 'With a few others of my regiment, I advanced from traverse to traverse until we secured an advanced position on the parapet of the fort . . .' "

address as Portland, Maine, had written letters to winners of the Congressional Medal of Honor in the Civil War asking them to describe in their own words how they had won the medal. It was Otis' dream that the personal stories of all those who had been awarded the medal would be published in book form.

James Otis was thorough and methodical in his search for the

—*Wood engraving from* Frank Leslie's Illustrated Newspaper, *depicting the assault on Fort Fisher, North Carolina, January 15, 1865*

facts. He sent to each a form, asking him to list his residence, occupation, place and date of birth, date of enlistment, record of service, battle participation, and finally (and most important) a brief description of the service for which the medal was awarded. Otis also asked for a photograph, which he promised would be returned.

On the form provided him by Otis, John Wainwright noted that he had been born in Syracuse, New York, but, at the outbreak of the war, he had been living in West Chester, Pennsylvania. When Fort Sumter fell and President Abraham Lincoln issued a call for 75,000 volunteers for three months' service, Wainwright immediately enlisted in the 2nd Pennsylvania Infantry. In September, he reenlisted in the 97th Pennsylvania Infantry. It was over three years later, while he was in command of this regiment, as a first lieutenant, that he was wounded and then subsequently awarded the Medal of Honor for gallantry in action.

Wainwright's modesty in recounting his part in the assault on Fort Fisher is typical of the replies received by James Otis. Very few of those who answered could be accused of overestimating their contribution.

In addition, it is quite obvious from the tenor of their replies that many of these veterans thought they were writing to another veteran of the war for whom long explanations or descriptions would be unnecessary. In fact, James Otis had not served in either the Army or the Navy. At the time of the Civil War he had been a boy in school. Only a very few of those who wrote to Otis seem to have recognized his name as that of a famous author whose pen name was James Otis, but whose full name was James Otis Kaler. The book for which he is best known is *Toby Tyler, or Ten Weeks with a Circus.*

The Congressional Medal of Honor is now our nation's highest award for valor, but during the Civil War it was the only medal given by the United States to her armed forces. And, at the beginning of the war, there was no medal at all. Near the end of the Revolution General George Washington had awarded a medal called the Purple Heart to three soldiers, but its use had then been discontinued.

The Civil War began on April 12, 1861, with the bombardment of Fort Sumter, South Carolina, but it was not until December 1861 that a bill was passed by both houses of Congress, and approved by President Abraham Lincoln, establishing a Medal of Honor to be awarded by the Secretary of the Navy to enlisted men. The Army medal was not authorized for enlisted men until July 1862. Then in March 1863 the law was amended to include Army officers also. Naval officers did not become eligible for the award until just prior to World War I.

Today, in a country that has often been accused of giving away far too many medals, one wonders why it took so long to establish a medal for the armed forces. What was the opposition, or objection, to the awarding of medals and decorations? An explanation would appear to be necessary. Many of our Founding Fathers were strongly of the opinion that titles, decorations, and medals were un-American, too European, and smacked strongly of an aristocracy. Their feelings were so strong on the subject that, when the Constitution was written, it contained a provision that: "No title of nobility shall be granted by the United States: and no person holding any office of profit or trust under them shall, without the consent of the Congress, accept of any present, emolument, office, or title of any kind whatever from any king, prince, or foreign state."

This took care of any foreign decorations but the same feeling of distrust prevailed toward American decorations or medals. Even as late as the 1890's, when James Otis was writing to some of the recipients of the Civil War Medal of Honor, he received replies indicating a feeling that these medals were a peculiar innovation for the people of this democratic country.

Perhaps the clearest expression of opinion on the subject came in a reply from Henry T. Johns of Philadelphia, who wrote, "Don't make a hero of me. I don't believe in this medal business." Here it should be noted that Mr. Johns, who had served in a Massachusetts regiment, received his award in November 1893 for bravery at Port Hudson, Louisiana, in May 1863. Thirty years had gone by between the deed and the recognition thereof.

Such lapses of time were not uncommon. The awarding of medals was something new to the men in the armed forces; they had to accustom themselves to the idea. Many brave deeds went unrewarded either because it never occurred to the witnesses to recommend a medal, or perhaps they simply did not believe in the whole idea. Several years might then elapse before someone sent in a recommendation, or perhaps the man himself might apply, particularly if he learned that someone else had been given the medal for the same deed, at the same time and place. In general the Navy Department was far more prompt in making awards. The Army had a much higher percentage of its medals issued long after the event.

Furthermore the wording of the Congressional acts establishing the medals was far from specific. The Secretary of the Navy was authorized to bestow the medal "upon such petty officers, seamen, landsmen, and marines as shall most distinguish themselves by their gallantry in action and other seamanlike qualities during the present war." The "other seamanlike qualities" paved the way for liberal presentations by officers who were inclined toward generosity. The act authorizing the Army medal was similarly vague in its wording.

Despite the fact that the Navy medal came first, the Army made the first awards. On March 25, 1863, the Secretary of War presented six medals to soldiers who had taken part in the Andrews Raid, an attempt to capture a railroad train in enemy territory, then run it northward destroying bridges between Chattanooga, Tennessee, and Atlanta, Georgia. There have been very few awards in the long history of the Congressional Medal of Honor that have attracted quite so much attention, and the story of "The Great Locomotive Chase" has continued to fascinate generation after generation of readers. Nine days later, the first Navy Medals of Honor were awarded to sailors who had participated in the bombardment of Forts Jackson and St. Philip guarding the mouth of the Mississippi River. Operations against these forts early in the morning of April 24, 1862, resulted in the capture of the city of New Orleans.

Today people think of the Congressional Medal of Honor as an award given for action involving actual conflict with an enemy, distinguished by gallantry and intrepidity at the risk of life above and beyond the call of duty; and today a great number of the awards are given posthumously. This was certainly not the way it was in the beginning. Medals in the Civil War were designed as badges of honor to be worn for people to see. The idea of posthumous awards had not yet taken hold. As a result there were practically none issued. Many of the most heroic deeds in our history performed in combat by personnel of the armed forces have never received any such recognition, and of course, since the Confederacy had no medal of honor, southern men were not awarded anything of the sort. Thus the names of many who today would have received this nation's highest tribute have been forgotten.

On the other hand there are inscribed on the rolls of the Medal of Honor the names of several who would not by today's standards have received this award. In its place they would have been given some lesser decoration. But there was no Distinguished Service Medal, no Distinguished Service Cross, no Navy Cross, no Silver Star or Legion of Merit, nor a Distinguished Flying Cross, Air Medal, Bronze Star or Purple Heart, not even a Good Conduct Medal. For bravery or other exemplary conduct deserving recognition, it was the Medal of Honor, or no medal at all. Thousands upon thousands of soldiers and sailors fought for three or four years and left the service with no decoration of any kind. The man who received a medal during the Civil War was the exception rather than the rule.

By comparison with the number of medals awarded to personnel of the armed forces in, for example, World War II, the number issued in the War Between the States was minute. With few exceptions, the soldier or sailor who received an award during the Civil War was deserving of some decoration by today's standards, if not the Medal of Honor perhaps the Silver Star or the Bronze Star. Thus the replies that James Otis received do not always describe exploits of extreme daring and bravery above and beyond the call of duty. This is fortunate because otherwise the letters would not contain such a great variety of stories. The collection, which is now the property of Charlie Kohen, even contains letters written by ex-soldiers who, at a later date, were to have their medals taken away from them.

The trouble was that there was no one charged with seeing that these new-fangled decorations were issued according to an established policy. As a result some mistakes were made. In 1916 an Army board of five retired general officers was appointed for the purpose of investigating and reporting upon past awards. The Navy Department did not appoint a similar board, but the Army reviewed all its Medals of Honor that had been issued up to that time.

The board discovered that, in the critical days just preceding the Battle of Gettysburg, when the tour of duty of the soldiers of the 27th Maine Volunteer Infantry was about to expire, President Abraham Lincoln had authorized issuing medals to any of its members who would volunteer to reenlist. Over three hundred men had decided to do so. Today these men would probably have received the Good Conduct Medal. One of these ex-soldiers, who never dreamed that some day his name would be stricken from the Medal of Honor list, wrote James Otis:

"The seductive part of your invitation is that it requests me to tell the tale myself. It is always a privilege to tell one's own story, but mine is really so unimportant that only a purpose to treat your kindness with due courtesy leads me to consent.

"It is stipulated at the outset that you use it just 'as it's writ,' no more is necessary and no less will do.

"Well, it so chanced when the war got well under way, your correspondent was rather a small boy way down in Maine with a big idea of patriotism and mightily interested in the great cause of Union versus Secession. June 1863 found my regiment, the 27th Maine Volunteers, camped near the old field of Bull Run, and during the latter days of that month our term of service expired. We had seen no battle, and during all those waning days of June, the Army of the Potomac swarmed about us on its way to the most celebrated contest of the war [Gettysburg]. It was a momentous juncture, a supreme occasion when specified terms of service, mere words of contract, should give way to the nobler spirit of the true soldier.

"The whole nation was alarmed and aroused. The boys from everywhere were marching toward Cemetery Hill and Little Round Top. We were clamoring to go home.

"The young blood of patriotism and inexperience in our regiment was hot and rebellious at the idea of running away while a great fight—it might be a decisive one—was pending. But a large portion of the regiment were men of family and business responsibilities. They had served their time and they wanted their quittance, glory or no glory. I do not know if I now blame them very much.

"When we were finally ordered to join the grand old column of the Army of the Potomac there was growling and protest. Then the War Department, recognizing the fact that the legal obligation of service had expired, revoked the order and called for volunteers to stay till the fight was over.

"A company or two, mostly of the younger men, remained, hoping to face fire in the great struggle now so plainly at hand. Of this we finally failed and, after Gettysburg was fought and won, returned home and were mustered out.

"I do not suppose men ever wanted to go into action more than we did, and it was for our offer to do so after our term expired that we were awarded the Medal of Honor.

"Not a great thing to do. Perhaps not, yet putting your head into the lion's mouth is all the same when making up your mind to try it, whether the lion chews it off or not. You do take an ugly chance.

"After getting out of service, like Mr. Finnigan, the most of us at once 'got in agin.' Some laid down heroic lives in later battles, many still later fell of their old wounds by the weary wayside, and others, God bless them, still live with honorable scars to doubly justify their title to the Medal.

"But I venture to say that, after their first battle, none were ever so anxious as in June '63 to get into a fight. Some people profess to like crow, but nobody hankers after it.

"As to my further part in that glorious war for liberty's last hope in the world, I rejoined the service, had ample battlefield experience, was discharged for disability in January 1865, and received a brevet majority for meritorious services. 'A shot horse is soon cured.' That is all."

Unfortunately medals had been awarded to every man of the regiment, whether he reenlisted or not. The board struck all 864 names from the list and then discovered another group award, but a much smaller one. This was a particularly poignant case:

"I was one of 24 first sergeants who were detailed as escort to the remains of President Lincoln in April 1865 and was with the escort from Washington to Springfield, Illinois.

"I was one of the eight who laid his body in the vault at Springfield. After our return we were ordered to report to the War Department and were presented with the medal by Adjutant General E. D. Townsend. I did not earn the Medal by capturing a battle flag or anything of that kind, but am conscious of the honor conferred upon me as one of this escort and consider it one of the grandest events of my life."

The names of all the especially selected men who had been chosen as the escort for the remains of President Lincoln were also stricken from the list.

The board then found a few individual cases where the medal had not been properly awarded. Among them was the only woman ever to receive the medal, Doctor Mary Walker. Since she had not been in the Army but, according to the board, "was a contract surgeon whose service does not appear to have been distinguished" her name was dropped from the rolls. Then, much to its regret, the board was forced to remove from the list the names of some very famous and undeniably brave men who had served as civilian scouts with the Army during the Indian Wars. The most outstanding name, whose removal from the list must have come as a shock to the public, was that of William F. "Buffalo Bill" Cody.

A total of 911 names were stricken from the list but the final conclusion of the board was that there had been "but few instances where the Medal had not been awarded for distinguished services."

For the period from 1861 to the beginning of World War I, there are on the rolls 1,723 awards of the Army Medal of Honor to 1,718 men. There were five men who received two awards of the medal.

For the same period the Navy Department awarded 731 medals to 722 men. There were nine men, including two marines, who won the Navy medal twice.

Thereafter the regulations were changed so that not more than one medal could be issued to one person. Then five enlisted men of the Marine Corps who had been awarded the Army Medal of Honor for service with the brigade assigned to the Army's 2nd Division in World War I were also given the Navy medal for the same service. There have been no other double awards since that time.

During the Civil War period only two sailors won the Navy medal twice, and there is no room for doubt that their awards were well deserved. The first of these was John Cooper who, at the famous Battle of Mobile Bay on August 5, 1864, was serving as coxswain on board the U.S.S. *Brooklyn*. The Navy Department General Order lists Cooper as having been born in Ireland in 1832 and then entering the service from New York State. Both of his citations for valor are dramatic:

FIRST AWARD

"On board the U.S.S. *Brooklyn* during action against rebel forts and gunboats and with the ram *Tennessee,* in Mobile Bay, 5 August 1864. Despite severe damage to his ship and the loss of several men

" '. . . *Cooper fought his gun with skill and courage throughout the furious battle . . .' "—The Battle of Mobile Bay, August 5, 1864*

(U.S. NAVY)

on board as enemy fire raked her decks from stem to stern, Cooper fought his gun with skill and courage throughout the furious battle which resulted in the surrender of the prize rebel ram *Tennessee* and in the damage and destruction of the batteries at Fort Morgan."

SECOND AWARD

"Served as quartermaster on Acting Rear Admiral Thatcher's staff. During the terrific fire at Mobile on 26 April 1865, at the risk of being blown to pieces by exploding shells, Cooper advanced through the burning locality, rescued a wounded man from certain death, and bore him on his back to a place of safety."

It seems most appropriate and in keeping with the highest traditions of the naval service that the second man to win the Navy medal twice should also have it awarded for gallantry while serving a gun under enemy fire, and secondly for saving another person's life at the risk of his own. Patrick Mullen was a boatswain's mate on the U.S.S. *Don* in the spring of 1865. On March 17, during an expedition to clear the region of Mattox Creek, Virginia, the boat crews encountered an accurate devastating fire from the shore. In the words of the Navy citation: "Rendering gallant assistance to his commanding officer, Mullen, lying on his back, loaded the howitzer and then fired so carefully as to kill and wound many rebels causing their retreat."

On May 1, the boat crews were again searching the same waters. In the meantime the surrender at Appomattox had occurred so there was little chance of encountering enemy action. Almost all southerners were abiding by the decision of General Lee to seek peace. Those who had not yet surrendered would soon follow his example. On this expedition Mullen's award was won for non-combat action:

"Engaged in picking up the crew of picket launch No. 6, which had swamped, Mullen, seeing an officer who was at that time no longer able to keep up and was below the surface of the water, jumped overboard and brought the officer to the boat, thereby rescuing him from drowning, which brave action entitled him to wear a bar on the medal he had already received at Mattox Creek, 17 March 1865."

The one Army man who was awarded the medal twice for his service in the Civil War had a very famous name. He was Second Lieutenant Thomas W. Custer. Both of his medals were won for the capture of Confederate flags but Lieutenant Custer was unable to write about his deeds. He had perished bravely in the desperate fighting with his older brother, George Armstrong Custer, at the Battle of the Little Big Horn in 1876.

But one of the most highly prized items in Charlie Kohen's collection is the reply received from Frank D. Baldwin.

It was not immediately apparent that this officer was one of the very few who had been awarded the Army medal twice. Baldwin had simply filled out the form James Otis had sent him and returned it with some newspaper clippings that mentioned his bravery in action at Peachtree Creek, Georgia, in July 1864. In fact, the newspaper articles he chose to send dealt mainly with the big Army shooting competition to be held at Fort Sheridan, Illinois.

"It was not immediately apparent that this officer was one of the very few who had been awarded the Army medal twice."—By the 1890's Captain Frank D. Baldwin had finally worked his way up to captain again.
(KOHEN COLLECTION)

Baldwin was the officer in charge and seemed more interested in publicizing this affair than in telling about his Civil War record. Furthermore he never mentioned, nor did the newspaper clippings, his second award when, in Texas in 1874, he had rescued two girls from Indians.

If one may be permitted to speculate, Frank Baldwin's failure to describe in detail what he had accomplished so many years before could have been due in part to the fact that nearly thirty years had passed before he had received his award. July 1864, when he had been a young captain of twenty-two and had led his company in a charge over the enemy breastworks and had, single-handed, captured two officers and a guidon, must have seemed a very long time ago. Thereafter for many years he had served his country on the western plains, where he had been associated with and fought alongside many ex-Confederates who had enlisted in the Army. Service on the Indian frontier had not always been very rewarding, certainly not in the matter of promotions. Due to the reduction in the size of the Army, he had been only a first lieutenant when he had won his second Medal of Honor in Texas in 1874. Now by the 1890's he had finally worked his way up to captain again.

One wonders if he knew that he was not the only Regular Army man who had suffered a reduction in rank before winning a second award. In the Indian Wars Sergeant Patrick Leonard had been awarded one in 1870 and then, as corporal, had been cited again for gallantry in action in 1876.

It was almost a certainty that some of our country's first medals would have been won by men who had served in famous units that had acquired well-deserved reputations for courage and fortitude in battle. One of the letters came from an Irish immigrant who had served with two immortal units. At the First Battle of Bull Run he had been with that New York regiment that was to win the nickname of the Fighting 69th. Later, in September 1861, James Quinlan was commissioned as a major in the 88th New York Infantry, one of the regiments of the famous Irish Brigade. It was in this capacity that he was serving when the 88th took part in the Battle of Savage's Station on June 29, 1862, one of the series of battles known to history as the Seven Days' Battle.

James Quinlan wrote: "I send you a true copy of General W. W. Burns' letter to the Secretary of War recommending me for the medal. By so doing I cannot be accused of egotism. I kept his original letter and had a typewritten copy made which the general signed and forwarded."

General Burns's letter begins with a description of the battle and then tells of the part played by the 88th New York and by Major Quinlan, who was commanding the regiment on that day.

"When I heard loud cries from my rear I thought the Rebels had turned me, but I was relieved to hear, in answer to my inquiry, that they were Major Quinlan and the 88th New York. I immediately formed this regiment facing the opening made in our ranks by the enemy battery firing down the Williamsburg Road. When they had discharged a volley, I sent the 88th at a charge up the road. The gallant Irishmen dashed forward with tremendous noise, and as the Confederate battery commander said in his report 'overwhelmed his battery, so that he had to limber up and retire precipitately.'

"The conduct of Major Quinlan on that occasion was that of a self-sacrificing soldier. He dashed into the very face of death. . . . Quinlan deserves *The Badge of Gallantry* to be awarded to the most brave and intrepid on the field."

General Burns's choice of words was most appropriate. In this period of our history, the Congressional Medal of Honor was the *only* badge of gallantry awarded to men in uniform.

The Passing Years

MORE than three hundred Union veterans answered the requests for their stories. From such a large group it can be expected that the replies would differ widely. The result is a uniquely fascinating collection. Some of the veterans simply filled out the forms sent them, putting in only part of the information requested. Others sent in typewritten replies going into great detail. But the majority of the letters are handwritten and vary from an almost illegible scrawl, undertaken in a clearly painful effort to overcome a handicap of little or no formal education, to graceful, beautifully formed script rarely seen today.

More often than not modesty was the keynote. Rather than talk about themselves, many of the winners of the medal referred to specific parts of the official records of the war, or to regimental histories where their exploits were recorded. A favorite device employed was to write the story of their wartime service in the third person, as if someone else were recording their deeds for posterity. Several sent newspaper clippings, thus letting a reporter tell their story for them.

In some cases other sections of the enclosed news clippings describing the events of the day compete in interest with the battle stories, and the prices given in the advertisements attached are sometimes wonderful to behold. A druggist located on Market Street in Wheeling, West Virginia, offered in *The Intelligencer,* rye whiskey at $1 a quart, or six quarts for $5, proclaiming: "When you send for a physician and he prescribes some whiskey, you should get only the very best."

A perusal of the office stationery used demonstrates more clearly than words that courage in battle has nothing whatever to do with a man's occupation in civilian life. Doctors, lawyers, a wig and toupee maker who imported fine French hair goods, clothing sales-

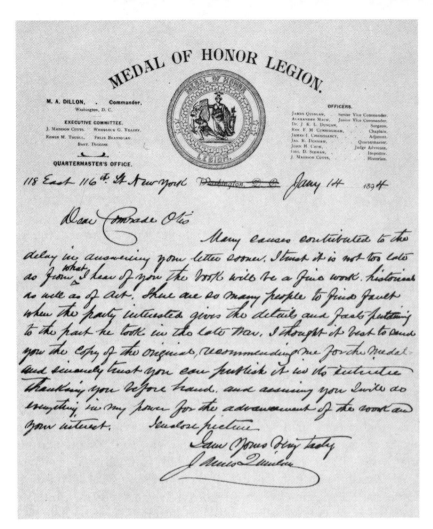

"Many of those who decided to answer at length chose stationery identifying them with veterans' organizations."

(KOHEN COLLECTION)

men, and boatmen, all were identified by their business letterheads.

Many of those who decided to answer at length chose stationery identifying them with veterans' organizations. Some of these letterheads were very decorative, took up a large part of the top of each sheet, and are worth saving for themselves alone as memorabilia of the times.

A Navy veteran who wrote about himself in the third person chose for his stationery the reverse side of a printed form letter somewhat opposed in spirit to the advertisement quoted above.

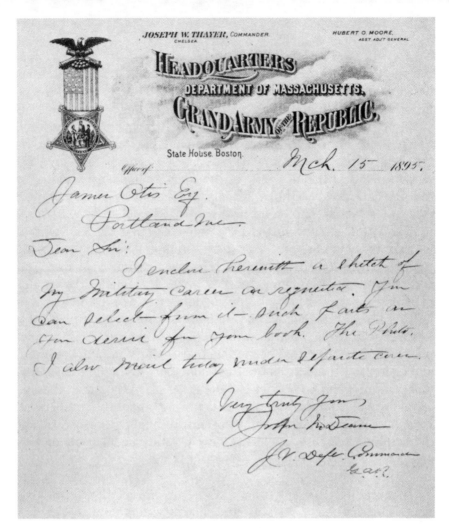

HEADQUARTERS
DEPARTMENT OF MASSACHUSETTS,
GRAND ARMY OF THE REPUBLIC,

State House, Boston.

Mch. 15— 1895.

James Otis Esq.

Portland Me—

Dear Sir:

I enclose herewith a sketch of my Military career as requested. You can select from it such facts as you desire for your book. The Photo, I also mail today under separate cover.

Very truly yours

John McSwearn

J. V. Dept Commander

&c.?

"Some of these letterheads were very decorative . . ."

It identified the writer as being "duly authorized to solicit and collect funds for the prohibition campaign of 1884."

Another intriguing bit of stationery came from Chicago imprinted, "Hooley's Theatre, The Parlor House of Comedy." This letter came from a veteran who had particularly distinguished himself for extreme gallantry at Vicksburg.

It seems most appropriate that a person who has taken such a tremendous interest in veterans' affairs as Charlie Kohen should be the one to acquire such a unique collection and, at the same time, be so well equipped by training and experience to recognize its historical value. In the thirty years since the collection became his property, he has given away only eight of these letters: one each to President Roosevelt, President Truman, the National Archives, the B'nai B'rith, Syracuse University, one museum and two historical societies. But in every case he has retained a photostat so that the collection would be, for all practical purposes, as complete as it was when he purchased it.

The letter donated to Syracuse University was the one written by John Wainwright, quoted at the beginning of this book, and the sequel to the gift produced a surprising coincidence. Wainwright had failed to send a photograph. Mr. John S. Mayfield, the curator of manuscripts and rare books for the university, asked Kohen, hopefully, if he could somehow find a photo to go with the letter. At a loss where to begin, Charlie picked up the Washington, D.C., telephone directory, selected at random one of the Wainwrights listed, and dialed the number. As Charlie remembers it, the first voice was that of a lady who said, "You had better speak to the admiral." The second voice announced, "You are talking about my father." A splendid photograph was obtained and, through the generosity of the admiral, Syracuse University now has the medal itself on display.

It is readily apparent from a study of some of the letters that James Otis had considerably more difficulty obtaining replies and cooperation from some of the veterans than Kohen had in obtaining the Wainwright photograph. A Detroit lawyer was just too busy to answer right away. He explained: "I have received two letters from you in relation to procuring the personal story of 'How I won the Medal of Honor during the Civil War.' I intended answering sometime ago, but the matter slipped my mind."

Andrew J. Widick, who enlisted at Decatur, Illinois, and had been decorated for heroism at Vicksburg in May 1863, then later moved to Elwood, Nebraska, had a better excuse: "I never heard of the granting of those medals until last spring, in March I think, and I received it in July. . . . I would have answered you sooner."

Former sergeant Francis Marion Cunningham of the 1st West Virginia Cavalry admitted that he hadn't intended to answer but finally relented only because "my children have been teasing me to do it." Also:

"I was not aware that my daughter had sent you any statement about my winning the Medal of Honor although I remember her asking me some questions about the matter some time ago. But I did not tell her all about it as there were some things that I did not care to tell my children. And perhaps what facts she has given you she has gotten from some of my comrades who were with me through the war. I believe that she has some statement of that particular affair written by two or three of my comrades. . . .

"I do not wish to speak or write about myself but, if your book is published, I would like to have the facts of my record stated as nearly correctly as possible. I will therefore send you with the photograph my own version of the matter. You can embellish the rough statement to suit yourself. I hope that you may be amply rewarded for your labor in the preparation of your book. Surely many of our brave comrades whose shoulders were never decorated with Eagles or Stars or even the shoulder strap of a 2nd Lieutenant—a Corporal or a Sergeant—but who have been counted worthy to receive the decoration of the Medal of Honor should have a place in the history of our bravest American soldiers."

Another who wished the author well, although he contributed little to the book, was former captain William Ludgate of the 59th New York Infantry. He wrote: ". . . for gallant services performed at Farmville, Virginia, April 7, 1865. I participated in the First Battle of Bull Run, July 21, '61 and was in nearly all the battles of the Army of the Potomac. I have not time to go into the details for which the medal was granted. In fact I do not care about repeating the facts. . . . I hope your book will prove a success in every way."

A most remarkable reply was received from Richard Stout, who hailed originally from Oswego, New York, had served in the Navy, and was living in Brooklyn in the 1890's. His ship, the U.S.S. *Isaac Smith*, had become trapped on the Stono River near Charleston, South Carolina, and forced to surrender. The U.S. Navy Department citation read, in part: "Carrying out his duties bravely through this action, Stout was severely wounded and lost his right arm while returning the rebel fire." Richard Stout simply recorded, "Lost right arm, received hip and neck wounds, confined in Charleston and Libby Prisons," and then explained that he believed "a man who vaunts personal deeds a cad."

Lewis A. Grant, who by the 1890's had become Assistant Secretary of War, had been given a Medal of Honor for "Personal gallantry and intrepidity displayed in the management of his brigade and in leading it in the assault in which he was wounded," at Salem Heights on May 3, 1863 (an action that formed a part of the larger Battle of Chancellorsville). He suggested that someone else ought to describe the service for which his medal had been awarded. He particularly stressed the courage shown by the men of his brigade, "usually known as the Old Vermont Brigade," and clearly conveyed his deep appreciation for the bravery of his men. He left the distinct impression that it was they, rather than any personal courage of his own, who had saved the day from ending in disaster.

Many officers and noncommissioned officers gave credit to their men but one cavalryman presented a particularly unusual reason why he himself did not deserve the prominence that had come his way for capturing three Confederate officers at Cedar Creek on October 19, 1864. "If there was any credit for the performance," he explained, "it was due entirely to my horse, the fastest in the company."

There was one group of people who either failed to respond to the letters they received or, more probably, were not sent any letters at all. These were the prominent public figures of the day whose exploits were so well known to almost everyone that James Otis perhaps saw no necessity to include them in his book. Therefore he may have considered that a recital of their deeds would not be news to his readers.

Lieutenant General John M. Schofield, the commanding general of the Union forces at the Battle of Franklin, Tennessee, which was fought on November 30, 1864, would certainly have fallen in this category. He had received his medal as a major of infantry for gallantry while leading his regiment in a charge at Wilson's Creek, Missouri, on August 10, 1861. After the war he had served as Secretary of War, as superintendent at West Point, and, at the time these letters were being written, was commanding general of the United States Army.

Daniel E. Sickles, corps commander who had lost a leg at Gettysburg, minister to Spain, prominent congressman, certainly also fell in this category, as did the famous one-armed general, Oliver O. Howard, former chief commissioner of the Freedman's Bureau, one of the founders of Howard University, Indian campaigner, and superintendent at West Point.

Then there was General Nelson A. Miles who had been decorated for bravely holding his position against repeated assaults at Chancellorsville. Although famous throughout the Army for many outstanding achievements, Miles was best known to the public as the officer who had been in command of the troops when the Indian chief Geronimo had surrendered. Later, Lieutenant General Miles succeeded Schofield as commanding general of the Army and held that post during the Spanish-American War. As such, he personally planned and led the expedition that resulted in the capture of Puerto Rico.

In the early 1890's there was another officer whose name was so well known in the United States that there seemed to be no need to ask him to write his story of how he had won the medal, but it is unfortunate that he was not asked to do so. For there is only one instance in the history of this country where both father and son have been awarded the Medal of Honor: the father in the Civil War, the son in World War II.

By 1864, the 24th Wisconsin had become one of the most famous regiments in the Civil War and its colonel, at nineteen, the youngest officer to hold that rank in the Union Army. The year before, on November 25, 1863, at the Battle of Missionary Ridge,

". . . there is only one instance in the history of this country where both father and son have been awarded the Medal of Honor . . ."
—Arthur MacArthur as a major general in the Philippines
(U.S. SIGNAL CORPS, NATIONAL ARCHIVES)

he had been a first lieutenant and regimental adjutant. At a critical moment he had seized the colors and shouting "On Wisconsin" had led the charge up the ridge and planted the flag at the top of the crest for all to see and follow. Arthur MacArthur subsequently joined the Regular Army, became well known and admired for his work in the Philippines, then retired as a lieutenant general. But his son, following in his footsteps, became far more famous. As all the world knows, General of the Army Douglas MacArthur's Medal of Honor was won on Bataan for conspicuous leadership, gallantry, heroic conduct, and utter disregard of personal danger, inspiring his troops and galvanizing the spirit of resistance of the Filipino people.

These were the men whose names are recorded in the history books, but what about the others who served their country so well that they were awarded its highest decoration? Today this government takes far better care of its veterans than it did in the years following the Civil War. What then did fate hold in store for those young men who had gone forth so bravely to fight for their country? How did they fare through the passing years?

Thomas F. Ellsworth carefully filled out the form sent him, recording his birthplace as Ipswich, Massachusetts, and the fact that he had enlisted in Boston in August 1862. Two years later Ellsworth had been promoted through the various enlisted ranks until he had been commissioned a lieutenant. In the battle fought at Honey Hill, South Carolina (near Savannah, Georgia), on November 30, 1864, he had saved the life of his regimental commander. For his heroism on this occasion, undertaken at the risk of his own life, through a murderous fire of grape, canister, and bullets at short range, Ellsworth had, over thirty years later, been awarded the Medal of Honor. Something else had also happened to him that must have been very disturbing to his peace of mind and his hopes of supporting a family. Thomas Ellsworth made no mention of it but one of the news clippings he sent noted that he had been discharged for wounds and physical disability incurred in the line of duty, but that he was now unemployed after twenty-five years in the Boston Customs House. He had lost his place and the only reason for the change was to make room for a member of the political party in power.

Another man did, however, express a complaint while apologizing for delaying his reply: "I am rather derelict in these matters and perhaps indifferent from being disgusted at the way Medal of Honor men and soldiers generally are treated by the government which they saved."

A different complaint was registered by a man who had saved the colors of his regiment in June 1864 in a hard-fought battle south of Petersburg. "Thousands of good soldiers fail in getting a pension for want of a hospital record and there is where the deadbeat and the hospital bummer are always ahead. Good honest soldiers, who would do almost anything rather than go to sick call and the hospital for a few days, are now suffering from the want of such a record, while the deadbeat who was always coming up with a stomach ache and getting excused from duty, managed to get into a hospital long enough to obtain a record. He is now enjoying a pension as he stumps around at reunions as an old battle-scarred veteran."

In complete and utter contrast to the "deadbeat . . . with a stomach ache" who in later years was all too prone to exaggerate his contributions, there were two letters from Charles D. Copp, a New Hampshire man cited for heroism at the Battle of Fredericksburg. The first letter listed the battles in which his regiment had participated. Then he realized that this list implied that he had personally fought in all of them. In his second letter Copp hastened to correct this impression. He wanted to make it clear that he had not been present in every battle and carefully noted those he had missed.

We may safely assume that those soldiers who had been severely wounded in battle must have been feeling the effects of their wounds in later years. A letter indicative of this fact was written on February 5, 1894, and mailed from Clayton, Jefferson County, New York. It was written on stationery imprinted "Dewey House, Thousand Islands, River St. Lawrence, Rates, $1.50 per day, Single Meals, 50 cents," but the form filled out and enclosed with the letter gave the writer's address as 8 Prospect Place, New Haven, Connecticut. The letter read:

"Dear Sir:

"Your letter has been forwarded to me at this place. I have been sick for quite a while and cannot write much. Have filled out the blank and send you by the same mail a part of a New Haven paper of December 1892, marked, which may give you a little bit of my war history. The article was poorly written by the reporter (green hand at the business) and the parts of my war record that were most prominent were left out. But I don't care about that. Maybe I prefer it so rather than have the whole town read it, as I never sought fame, honor, or notoriety. Will send you a photograph taken in the summer of 1892. Please return the same when you are through with it.

"I don't care to tell of my own deeds. I always dreaded to. It seemed so egotistical, but you are welcome to all you can learn from the filled-out blank and the paper. You may make such use of the same as may seem most advisable to you.

"How much will the book be? And when will it be delivered? Please let me know.

"Fraternally yours,
"*Fred R. Jackson*"

The War Department citation gives enough of the facts to make it clear that this was a remarkable soldier indeed. "First Sergeant, Company F, 7th Connecticut Infantry; at James Island, S.C., 16 June, 1862; Having his left arm shot away in a charge on the enemy, he continued on duty, taking part in a second and a third charge until he fell exhausted from the loss of blood."

First Sergeant Jackson had enlisted at New Haven, Connecticut, at seventeen years of age. At James Island he had been only eighteen years old. Nor was this the end of his wartime career. On the form provided he recorded that he had been taken prisoner, been through six southern prisons, and had "graduated from Libby Prison on October 14, 1862."

The southern doctors must have taken good care of him but surgery in the nineteenth century left much to be desired, which means that Frederick R. Jackson must have had an iron constitution as well as a tremendous will to live and do his share in the war. For he also wrote that he took part in thirty-two battles during the war: "Five before I lost my arm and 27 afterwards. While I was an officer, I was very often sent to the front with special messages to the commanding generals, and remained until the fight was over, acting as a volunteer aide on their staff."

It will be noted that Sergeant Jackson wanted a copy of the book. A great number of these men, whether they wrote their own

" '. . . Having his left arm shot away in a charge on the enemy, he continued on duty, taking part in a second and a third charge until he fell exhausted from the loss of blood.' "—Wood engraving of the assault on James Island, South Carolina, June 16, 1862, from Frank Leslie's Famous Leaders and Battle Scenes of the Civil War

(FORT WARD MUSEUM, ALEXANDRIA, VIRGINIA)

stories or let a newspaper reporter tell it for them, asked for a copy, even those who had fallen upon hard times and could ill afford it, like the ex-soldier who asked, "Please write when your book is completed and give me a price list. If able, will buy one. Am poor and broken down, but will try for a book."

Some could not afford to have a photograph taken but a veteran who managed to do so added a postscript to his letter: "P.S. I have been to some necessary expense to have this written and also had to have my photograph taken expressly for you, so when the book is published I would like to have you send me a copy."

Although handicapped and suffering in some cases in their later years, these men asked for no sympathy because they may have been severely wounded, although one man, Sergeant Eri D. Woodbury of New Hampshire who had served in a Vermont cavalry regiment, would obviously have preferred being wounded earlier in his career. He told of winning his medal at Cedar Creek, then of being struck by a shell fragment the day before Appomattox and thereby losing the opportunity of "participating in the Great Parade in

Washington." Anyone who has ever read anything about this parade will understand why he felt this way. There has never been in the history of the United States anything comparable to it. On the first day came the Army of the Potomac, the blue columns led by Major General George G. Meade flowing by dense and rhythmic—80,000 strong. On the second day the Army of the Tennessee and the Army of Georgia swung down Pennsylvania Avenue, nearly 70,000 men, with Major General William Tecumseh Sherman at their head. They came with a longer stride, a different swing, but, to Sherman's surprise, marched superbly. A reporter from the New York *World* compared the two, calling the Army of the Potomac an army of citizens, the westerners an army of pioneers. Small wonder Sergeant Woodbury regretted his inability to take part; no one would ever see anything like this again. The modern quadrennial inaugural parades and the victory parades following our later wars pale by comparison with the accounts of this two-day march of 150,000 men.

These extracts from letters, and the stories that follow told in greater detail, provide significant glimpses into the minds and hearts of the brave men who fought for the North during the Civil War. It is most unfortunate that no similar collection could have been made of southern letters, but it seems safe to say that in many ways their letters would have been similar. Brave men fought on each side; the contest would not have been so prolonged if that had not been the case. In certain respects the southern letters would inevitably have been different; there would have been no talk of hospital records because there could have been no hope of pensions from a nonexistent government. The reasons why they fought would have been expressed differently, but there would probably have been no more mention of the word slavery in the southern letters than appears in the northern letters.

There would have been flashes of humor in the southern letters just as in the northern letters. One wonders what the Confederate soldiers ate, if anything, on the day a sergeant of the Pennsylvania Infantry wrote: "Marched all night as fast as they could drive us. In the morning as the sun rose, we turned off the road to our right. There the Army wagons stood, loaded with raw mackerel and throwed them out to us as we marched by." But as a New York cavalryman said, "As the years go by, one forgets the hardships and remembers the bright side."

III

Infantrymen in Battle

DURING our more recent wars, a great deal of money, time, and effort has been devoted to telling the public and, to a lesser extent, our soldiers why we fight. During the Civil War, or the War Between the States, the issue was clearcut. The war was being fought to determine whether or not a state had the right to secede. Furthermore, the symbols representing the cause for which the soldiers fought were there, prominently displayed, in the thick of battle, for all to see. Their country's flag, together with the regimental colors, was with them, entrusted to their care. No soldier had to be told why he fought; he could see the flag of his country flying proudly, and to be selected as a color bearer or as a member of the color guard was an honor not lightly bestowed upon an individual.

It is not surprising that many of the fiercest struggles of the war occurred while trying to save the flag, or to capture the enemy's. At sea, the striking or lowering of a ship's flag meant that the ship had surrendered. The loss of the colors on land did not mean that a unit had surrendered but, in the eyes of the men, the effect of losing a flag by capture was almost as great a disaster, something to be prevented at all costs. No matter how many brave color bearers were killed or wounded, others would spring forward to raise again the symbol for which each man fought. Furthermore, for many units, these flags also had a very personal meaning. They had been cut out and hand-sewn by mothers, wives, and sweethearts, then presented with due ceremony to the regiment, to be carried proudly in battle.

"Our army was defeated and, while falling back, the colors were in great danger of capture." James Madison Burns, enlisted at sixteen, a sergeant before he was eighteen, then a captain after over thirty years' service in the postwar Army, where promotions practically never occurred, was trying to describe his part in a battle fought on May 15, 1864, in the Valley of Virginia.

The battle he was recalling was one of the most famous of the war because of the participation of the cadets of the Virginia Military Institute. The Confederates had attacked and were driving the Union army before them. The colors of James Burns's own regiment, the 1st West Virginia Infantry, were in danger.

"Seeing this I rallied a few men. We started forward, and when in a good position, opened fire, drove the enemy back, and then started to the rear with the colors. Shortly after starting back, I heard a man calling to me that he was wounded. I immediately ordered the men to go on with the colors and I returned for the wounded man, who proved to be Travilla A. Russell of my own Company B, 1st West Virginia Volunteer Infantry. I was at the time a Sergeant. I assisted him up and off the field of battle thereby saving him from capture, as well as the flag of my regiment. This was all done under heavy fire. I never was under a heavier fire than I was for a few minutes at the time above described."

With his letter Burns enclosed a newspaper article that added something to the story. "His conduct received ringing cheers from the men of both armies who witnessed the brave deed."

The soldiers of both sides were well aware that their flags also exerted tremendous powers of attraction; they knew that their enemy was almost as eager to capture a flag as to preserve his own. On occasion, a unit might even use its flag to wave tauntingly at

" 'His conduct received ringing cheers from the men of both armies who witnessed the brave deed.' " —James M. Burns, a captain after over thirty years' service in the postwar Army (KOHEN COLLECTION)

the enemy, to dare him to try to take it. Such bravado was not always advisable; the flag could be lost that way. Captain Thomas J. Box of Bedford, Indiana, recorded an event illustrating this fact quite clearly. It occurred at Resaca, Georgia, on May 14, 1864, one day prior to the event just described by Captain Burns. The Battle of Resaca ended as a Union victory, the first in a long campaign fought between Sherman's three armies trying to reach Atlanta and Joseph E. Johnston's two armies striving to protect the approaches to the city.

"It was at the Battle of Resaca. Our regiment, the 27th Indiana, was advanced beyond the main line when we were suddenly charged by the enemy. We were commanded to reserve our fire until the Rebels were within thirty feet of us. When they came so near, we opened a terrible volley and charged with bayonets, driving the enemy back into their works. They fell back and formed a new line. We also fell back and formed on our old line. They charged up to our line again. We gave them another volley and broke their ranks.

"The Rebel colonel, Colonel Langford of the 38th Alabama, jerked the Rebel flag and waved it in front of my company. I passed the head of my company, telling my men to be careful how they shot. I went to the colonel, took hold of the flagstaff with my left hand. The colonel brought his sword down on the hilt of my sword and said to me, 'If you are going to surrender, go to the rear. You may get hurt here.'

"I said, 'No, I am after you.'

"At that moment, one of my men came up. I told him to shoot his [Colonel Langford's] brains out. The colonel gave me the flag and said he would surrender. I took him back to the rear of my command and turned him over. I was very highly complimented by General Williams and also by the colonel of my own Regiment."

The capture of a Confederate flag by John Lilley of Lewistown, Pennsylvania, led to a somewhat delicate officer–enlisted man situation. A soldier with lesser resolve to hold on to his prize of war might have given ground and lost recognition for the capture. Private John Lilley, Company F, 205th Pennsylvania Infantry, refused to do so. "When I got back a little distance, some lieutenant wanted me to give him the flag. I profanely declined and called his attention to the fact that there were plenty more flags over there where I got mine."

Private Lilley's flag capture had occurred on April 2, 1865, just a week before Appomattox. Prior to that time, however, assaults against fortifications had not been very successful. Corporal Francis E. Warren of Hinsdale, Massachusetts, who served in the 49th Massachusetts Infantry, wrote of an attack against Port Hudson, Louisiana, on May 27, 1863, which he described as "a forlorn hope." A call was made for volunteers to lead an assault. "This body of men was hastily and somewhat imperfectly organized, as it seemed, with a very poor record kept by the War Department. The men

" 'This body of men was hastily and somewhat imperfectly organized, as it seemed, with a very poor record kept by the War Department."—Francis E. Warren as a U. S. senator from Wyoming (KOHEN COLLECTION)

were to take fascines (made by binding branches and twigs together with grapevines, into bunches about eight feet long and one foot in diameter, weighing from 15 to 30 pounds each) in their arms, with shovels, in addition to the muskets on their backs. They were to march to the enemy's parapets or breastworks, cast their fascines in the outer ditch, at the same time leveling the works and filling the ditches so that the cannon and men might advance.

"The field to be passed over was a wilderness of fallen timber which had been burned over, consuming leaves, twigs and small limbs. The enemy's fire was so galling that the fascine bearers never reached the top, nearly all being killed or wounded before they had gotten half way across the field."

One suspects that his reference to "a very poor record kept by the War Department" means that he had some trouble obtaining his decoration, which was not issued to him until 1893. His criticism seems a bit unjust because complete, accurate rosters of volunteers participating in such an attack would not normally be kept. However, if he encountered some trouble, other less well-known persons must have had more, because by that time Francis E. Warren was a U.S. senator from Wyoming.

In this connection, when World War I was fought, his son-in-law, General John J. Pershing, insisted that recommendations for the Congressional Medal of Honor be submitted promptly and he personally reviewed each case. One cannot help but wonder if such action on the part of General Pershing could have been, in part, inspired by his father-in-law.

On June 14, 1863, two weeks after the first attack on Port Hudson, the Union army undertook another assault on the fortifications. This effort met the same fate, whereupon the northern troops settled down for a long siege, similar to that already under way farther up the Mississippi at Vicksburg.

On July 4, the day that Vicksburg finally surrendered, the Siege of Port Hudson was still in progress. Marcus A. Hanna, of South Portland, Maine, a sergeant in Company B, 50th Massachusetts Infantry, who had already served one enlistment in the Navy, described the situation confronting his company on that date.

"On July 4th, 1863, the Siege of Port Hudson had been in progress about six weeks. My company was in rifle pits supporting a battery within close range of the rebel works.

"The day was an intensely hot one and by noon every canteen was dry. Soon the men were all suffering from thirst. At about 2 p.m., Lieutenant Hurd, in command of the company, gave his consent for volunteers to go to the rear for water. Except for the orderly sergeant, I was the only sergeant present, and I felt that it devolved on me to go. I volunteered to make the trial, asking for two men to go with me. No one volunteered and Lieutenant Hurd would detail no one, so I resolved to make the try alone. No doubt the peril was less for one.

"After testing the Rebel aim and temper with a dummy raised on the edge of the pit, I collected about a dozen canteens, sprang from the pit and ran across the open plain to the rear. Rebel buckshot and bullets struck on all sides of me but I gained cover, about 1,000 yards away, without being hit. When half the distance had been gained I threw myself flat on the ground as if hit, which had the effect of causing the rebel fire to slacken. Reaching safe ground (a blackberry hedge well-remembered by the Port Hudson troops) I still had a good half-mile to go for the water.

"However, the enemy was more hospitable in their treatment of me on my return and I reached the pit again with my load of full canteens and a 'special' for Lieutenant Hurd which he doubtless remembers with pleasure."

The "hospitable . . . treatment" was undoubtedly the withholding of fire by the Confederates when they saw that Sergeant Hanna was bringing water to his comrades. Such chivalrous acts occurred frequently on both sides during this war between Americans.

It would seem that Marcus Hanna's heroic deeds did not end at the close of the war for, in addition to the letter quoted above, he wrote:

"The inscription on the gold life-saving medal awarded me when Keeper of the Cape Elizabeth Light is as follows:

'In testimony of heroic deeds in saving from the
perils of the sea.

'To Marcus A. Hanna for nobly saving two men
from the wreck of the schooner

—A U S T R A L I A—
January 28th, 1885' "

Beyond the Mississippi, in the year 1864, a spectacular northern failure occurred. From a strictly military point of view, the ill-fated Red River expedition should never have been attempted. From the northern point of view it accomplished nothing, and from the southern point of view it almost resulted in the complete capture of both a northern army and a northern fleet. The two most important battles fought in the campaign were the Battle of Sabine Cross Roads which the victorious Confederates called the Battle of Mansfield, fought on April 8, and the Battle of Pleasant Hill fought on April 9.

Sergeant John H. Cook of Company A, 119th Illinois Infantry,

wrote a description of the Battle of Pleasant Hill that is most unusual. The average soldier or junior officer has only a worm's-eye
view of any large battle. Generally he knows what he did and what
happened near him but very little else, unless he has an opportunity
and also takes the time to study the tactics later. Sergeant Cook,
who enlisted in Quincy, Illinois, but was born in London, England,
apparently did take time to study the details of this battle. In a
covering letter Cook admitted that he had written a similar description for Brigadier General T. H. Rodenbough's book, *The
Bravest Five Hundred of '61*, but he added that he had changed it
somewhat.

The changes were all to the good. The new account is not only
a clearer sketch, but it is also an excellent story of what actually
occurred on the battlefield that day, showing the initial success
gained by the attacking Confederates, as well as their ultimate
repulse. It will be noted by the careful observer that, although the
Confederate attack was thrown back, the Union army retreated
hastily at daybreak the next day.

In this connection, many students of the war contend that if
General Richard Taylor, who is one of the heroes of the state of
Louisiana, had been permitted to pursue the Union army after
Pleasant Hill both the Union army and the Union fleet would have
been captured.

In his covering letter, Sergeant Cook also wrote:

"I would like to see your book a success, beyond that I have no
personal vanity other than to satisfy a wish you would make your
article about me as brief and modest as you can. There are thousands more deserving of mention and more worthy of the medal,
though I am proud of my record of service and the medal which
I seldom display."

His unusually descriptive account follows, quoted in its entirety:

"Our command arrived at Pleasant Hill in the night after a hard
day's march. We expected to go into the fight the next morning,
and perhaps before daylight, for it was generally believed the Confederates would attack us, following up their victory of the day
before.

"I had served as a sergeant in my company for over a year when
I was detailed at Brigade Headquarters to assist the Brigade-
Quartermaster, and had performed my duties with him for several

months. But when there was fighting to do, what I enlisted for, it seemed to me that my place was with my company, and I was dissatisfied to be a non-combatant. I told Lieutenant Allen, our Brigade-Quartermaster, just how I felt and that my place was to report to my company for duty. He objected, but let me go.

"How well I can remember now, though it is more than thirty years ago, just how the boys received me as I reported to our captain and fell in as a file closer, as the company was formed for the skirmish line. All sorts of jibes and jeers greeted me for I had no accoutrements, except for a cartridge belt and a Sharp's breech-loading rifle: no haversack or canteen, no provisions, nothing but my gun, 'Forty Rounds,' and a plug of tobacco. But the boys were glad to see me in my old place, for I was always a favorite with them, as well as with my commanding officers.

"Our place was assigned on the extreme left of our line, as skirmishers. Our orders were to hold at a given point in the thick woods and to stubbornly resist any attack. Here we halted and remained from early in the morning until about 3 o'clock in the afternoon. Meanwhile the battle had been raging on the right flank of our army and repeated assaults, on both the right and centre, had been repulsed. We could see from our position, away out on the left, almost the whole of the battle.

"About 4 o'clock there was a lull. Confederate reinforcements had arrived and were preparing for a final charge, which should overwhelm us. Their plan was to break through our centre and flank us on our left. Suddenly a terrific charge was made, the enemy driving everything before them. The 13th and 19th Corps could not resist the overwhelming assault. Our centre broke and it seemed nothing could now stay the furious onslaught. They had passed to a point parallel with our skirmish line, away on the left, but had not yet struck the centre reserve, the grand old fighters of the 16th Corps.

"Meantime the attack began on our skirmish line in the woods, their purpose of flanking us being plainly seen, which would still further demoralize our centre.

"We had not been firing long when the command of our line fell on Lieutenant Ware, gallant soldier, he was! He ordered me to the company's front and centre and told me to lead the line right on through the brush, as though we were the attacking party with plenty of support. I was leading the line by some thirty or forty feet, and was a target for the enemy's fire. It seemed as though a hundred shots were focussed on me, and to advance was certain death, but I kept on, rapidly firing my breech-loader and moving further forward.

"Turning to see if our line was all right I saw the old pet and pride of our company, John MacIntyre, throw up his hands and fall. Running back to him, where three or four of the boys had gathered around him, I saw he was instantly killed. Then I was maddened. All thought of fear had vanished. I ran out in advance, with my empty gun, and waving my cap in the air yelled out, 'Come on boys!' It seemed to me as though I was going to destruc-

" 'I ran out in advance, with my empty gun, and waving my cap in the air yelled out, "Come on boys!" ' "—Newspaper sketch of Sergeant John H. Cook (KOHEN COLLECTION)

tion but I didn't care, for if we did not repulse those rebel flankers, panic would follow and all would be lost.

"Just then our skirmish line reserve became engaged through the heavy firing which passed through our thin line, and a volley from our rear came pouring through behind us. Here we were between two fires, our Orderly Sergeant being shot by our own brigade. Suddenly the main battle was turned, by the repulse of the onslaught on our centre. The enemy had struck our reserve, the 16th Corps, and met their Waterloo. It seemed less than a minute when our defeat was turned to victory. In the woods we took a number of prisoners, sending them to the rear and kept on moving forward until dark, but still separated from our regiment. We occupied an advanced position as pickets until near daylight when orders were given to retreat back to our fleet on the Red River.

"The next day I joined the Brigade Head Quartermaster. I was complimented by Lieutenant Ware on the field and, subsequently, both he and Lieutenant Allen recommended me for a 'Medal of Honor.' It came inscribed on the back 'The Congress to Serg't John H. Cook, Co. 'A,' 119th Ills. Inf'ty for conspicuous bravery, at the Battle of Pleasant Hill, La., Apr. 9th, 1864.' "

Sometimes in the history of warfare a small force, normally an integral part of a much larger unit, exerts an influence upon history out of all proportion to its size. When this happens it is almost invariably due to the presence of an individual who is an outstanding, determined leader of men.

In July 1864 Lieutenant General Jubal A. Early crossed the Potomac River and marched toward Washington. His purpose was to make a demonstration toward the northern capital to relieve the mounting pressure being applied by Grant's armies on Richmond and Petersburg. General Early's little army, when it started down the Shenandoah Valley, amounted to only about 14,000 men but reports concerning it greatly exaggerated the number of troops involved and caused tremendous excitement in Washington. Many feared for the safety of the Union capital.

On July 9, 1864, General Lew Wallace, commander of the Middle Department, made a stand at the Monocacy River, just southeast of Frederick, Maryland. He had with him only about 6,000 troops, many of whom were poorly trained for battle. General Wallace had no hope of stopping the Confederates, but it was his duty to delay their advance as long as he could, thus giving the officers responsible for the safety of Washington the maximum amount of time to prepare for its defense.

To guard the main road toward Washington, General Wallace stationed the majority of his best troops, a division of the Sixth Corps under the command of General Ricketts, on the near side of the river. On the far side, toward the advancing Confederates, he placed a small body of skirmishers with orders to defend the wooden bridge on the main road. They were to remain in position until further orders. Their mission was to delay, to gain as much time as possible, then retreat, burning the bridge behind them.

However, as the situation developed, when the Confederates saw that the direct approach to the bridge was blocked, they sent a flanking force to cross downstream. The main battle developed there, and when Jubal Early's army delivered a successful attack in that area, aiming toward the rear of the turnpike bridge, this left the defending force on the far side of the river exposed, with no chance to retreat as originally planned along the main road.

First Lieutenant George E. Davis, of Burlington, Vermont, was now in command of the small body of skirmishers. Other more senior officers had been present at the beginning of the battle but, for reasons which are not entirely clear, they had disappeared, leaving him in charge. Lieutenant Davis had enlisted as a private in the earliest days of the war. He was now an experienced combat veteran. The soldiers from his own unit, Company D of the 10th Vermont Infantry, were thoroughly reliable but his was a mixed, command and included a number of men whose combat efficiency was very questionable.

Many years later General Lew Wallace wrote a letter describing the event. In the intervening years he had become famous as the author of *Ben Hur* and the events of that July 9 were obviously very fresh in his memory. To describe the service for which he had been awarded the Medal of Honor, Lieutenant (later Captain) Davis furnished "a correct copy" of this letter written by Lew Wallace:

"Captain Davis was in command of our skirmishers on the west bank of the river, the main body being in line on the bluff forming the east-bank. The purpose of stationing him there was to defend the wooden bridge continuing the pike from Frederick City to Washington. I did not wish to burn the bridge unless it became absolutely necessary to do so. He crossed by it, going into position early in the morning.

"The enemy began the attack by a dash for the bridge, and was met by Captain Davis' skirmishers. General Ricketts and I watched the affair from a hill-top, and for a time were greatly concerned lest Davis' flank should be turned; but when we saw him retire his right, and form a half-circle around the west exit of the bridge, we became assured he was alert, and able to take care of himself. The stubborn resistance he offered, supported by a vigorous artillery fire from the heights, diverted the enemy from the bridge and compelled him to turn our position, for which he marched past Captain Davis to a ford down the river. It was not long until the Confederates appeared on the east bank. They lost no time in attacking us there, and their assault was decisive of the fate of the bridge. It had to go; and what was worse, it had to go leaving Davis and his whole detachment cut off and lost unless they could swim the river under close fire.

"I rode to see the order executed. Ricketts' line was engaged from wing to wing. Nearly thirty years have passed, yet I remember as if it were yesterday the struggle I had with myself to have the match applied. To burn the structure looked like a deliberate sacrifice of the gallant skirmishers—or rather like a wicked desertion. I argued: Ricketts may be driven before Davis can be retired; if I retire Davis, the enemy will follow on his heels; and then—and this nerved me—if the bridge was allowed to stand, Early would be en-route for Washington, it might be in an hour. *To save Davis was to lose Washington.* I gave the word, and in five minutes the eastern end of the old crossing was a whirl of flame and smoke. With a last look at my skirmish line—it was still fighting—I rode away."

General Wallace's statement *"To save Davis was to lose Washington"* was, in fact, an exaggeration. His opponent, General Early, knew that his small Confederate army could not possibly capture the northern capital; the defenses were far too strong, although the Union forces assigned to them had been weakened in order to strengthen Grant's armies besieging Richmond and Petersburg.

However, it is no exaggeration to say that it was essential to burn the bridge on the turnpike to slow the Confederate advance. When Early's men did appear in front of Washington they demonstrated briefly and created so much excitement that the legend still persists that Jubal Early was trying to capture the city. If the road had been left open, the bridge left intact, Early's troops would probably have created even more consternation than they actually did. One or more of the forts defending the city might have fallen. It is difficult to say how far the repercussions might have spread, or what effect might have been produced on the Union plans to end

" '. . . if the bridge was allowed to stand, Early would be en-route for Washington . . .' "—Sketch from Fighting for Time *by Glenn H. Worthington*

the war. Even without the capture of one or more forts, Early's raid on Washington accomplished its purpose of relieving the pressure on Richmond and Petersburg; General Grant moved a large number of Union troops northward from Richmond by water to try to capture General Early before he could return across the river to Virginia.

Let us return to Lieutenant Davis, with the bridge burning behind him, his own army disappearing in the distance, pursued by the victorious Confederates—his predicament can be easily imagined by anyone who visits the battlefield today. The present road bridge is located in the same place. Upstream, around a bend, a quarter of a mile away, are the tracks of the main line of the Baltimore and Ohio Railroad, crossing high over the river. And overlooking the whole scene of the action on both sides of the river are hills and ridges commanding the area where Davis and his men were pinned down. Lew Wallace's letter continues: "In the night succeeding, I heard that Davis and a portion of his men had escaped. . . . That he would attempt to cross the river by the railroad bridge, stepping from tie to tie, under fire at close range, and forty feet in the air, never occurred to my mind. It was one of the bravest things of the war. Riding off the field, I imagined him dead, or on the way to Libby; but now I put my hand on his shoulder and ask Vermont, the mother of so many men stout in their courage and loyalty, to do him honor."

" '. . . I . . . ask Vermont, the mother of so many men stout in their courage and loyalty, to do him honor.' "
—Captain George E. Davis, from a drawing in A History of the Tenth Regiment, Vt. Vols., *by Chaplain Edwin M. Haynes, D.D.*
(LIBRARY OF CONGRESS)

The War Department citation given to Lieutenant George E. Davis reads, "While in command of a small force, held the approaches to the two bridges against repeated assaults of superior numbers, thereby materially delaying Early's advance on Washington," and gives a fair idea of what happened.

On the other hand, the War Department citation for John M. Deane for bravery at Fort Stedman, Virginia, on March 25, 1865, gives no hint whatever of what preceded the event, so that the best part of the story would be missing if Deane had not written his version of the battle.

The last major attack of the Confederate Army of Northern Virginia was delivered just before dawn on March 25, 1865, against Fort Stedman, one of the main fortifications erected by the Union armies outside Petersburg. Captain Deane's regiment, the 29th Massachusetts Infantry, occupied a battery just south of Fort Stedman and on the main line between it and Fort Haskell. His citation reads: "This officer, observing an abandoned gun within Fort Haskell,

"The last major attack of the Confederate Army of Northern Virginia was delivered just before dawn on March 25, 1865, against Fort Stedman . . ."
—*Wood engraving,* Harper's Weekly

(FORT WARD MUSEUM)

called for volunteers, and, under a heavy fire, worked the gun until the enemy's advancing line was routed."

John M. Deane (brevetted major for gallant and meritorious service in this battle) wrote, from Fall River, Massachusetts, a much more interesting account:

"At the same time that the enemy entered and captured Stedman, a flanking party entered and captured a portion of the camp of the 29th Massachusetts. This capture included that part of the line held by my company. When I hastened from my quarters at the alarm, and jumped into the *trench* of the *main line,* I landed right into a company of rebels who had swarmed in over the breastwork, and were still coming in. I called: 'Who are you—the pickets driven in?'

"*It was very dark.* Captain Williams who commanded the next company heard my voice and hastily pushed to where I was and whispered: 'These are all Johnnies. Our companies are captured. Get out of this.'

"Just then I heard a voice and there was no mistaking it. It said: 'By God, boys, there is a good fat knapsack.'

"I held my sword closely to my leg and pushing along, elbow to elbow and shoulder to shoulder with the 'rebs,' got out of the trench and hastened across the camp to regimental headquarters and reported the condition of things on my part of the line. From the very much excited major in command, I received the order: 'Go back and hold your line!'

"After some sharp words with the major about the folly of his order, and a request for men to hold the line, I concluded I had better go slow as he was my superior officer, and we were in actual conflict with the enemy. I started back alone, armed only with a regulation sword. Reaching my part of the line I now saw but a single individual there; a bombproof was between us. We challenged each other three times. Neither would give his regiment. He was a very large man and had on dark clothes; I was satisfied he was not a member of my company. I moved to the right of the bombproof. He moved in the same direction and in the darkness we came face to face. He at once complied with my demand for surrender and handed me his *revolver*; he had no sword or belt. He was a captain in a North Carolina regiment. I returned to headquarters and reported that I had performed the duty assigned me, and that my part of the line was now clear of the enemy. I had several tilts with the major after this about the advisability of remaining 'to hold the line,' which meant capture as soon as the enemy chose to advance upon us from Stedman which he still held.

"When after daylight the enemy advanced upon Fort Haskell,

sweeping through our camp of course, I at the last moment leaped the breastworks, and called for all who did not wish to be captured to follow me, down between the main lines to Haskell. *All* followed me except the major, a captain, and the regimental surgeon. These three officers were of course taken out of their 'bombproof' and sent to Richmond.

"Arriving at Haskell, I performed the service for which the medal was awarded. As soon as General Hartranft charged upon the enemy and forced him to retreat, I left Haskell with the men of my regiment and pursued the enemy through our old camp, retaking it. I was just in time to overhaul a major of the 4th Georgia regiment, between the lines, and relieve him of his *revolver and belt*; he had no sword.

"The battle was now over and we reestablished ourselves in our old camp. The capture of the officers referred to left me in command of the regiment. I have the two revolvers and the belt now, which with 'a brevet' and a 'Medal of Honor' are more trophies than usually fall to the lot of one man in a single battle."

The War Department citation for Captain Marion T. Anderson is completely misleading. One cannot help but wonder if its wording was due to a misunderstanding in Washington of what happened at Nashville on December 16, 1864, or if the wording was intentional to conceal the true story from the public. The citation reads: "Led his regiment over five lines of the enemy's works, where he fell, severely wounded."

Writing from the cash room of the city post office in Washington, D.C., on January 8, 1894, Marion Anderson, who enlisted in Kokomo, Indiana, in response to President Lincoln's first call for volunteers, makes it very clear that the five lines in question were not enemy lines. Describing his part in the two-day Battle of Nashville, fought December 15 and 16, 1864, Anderson wrote:

"The first day's fight, the 51st Indiana, Anderson in command, was in the front line of his brigade. A charge was ordered and like a whirlwind did they go, on and up, until the enemy's works were scaled and carried. The second line was also carried, and again, in the afternoon, a third line of works was charged and carried. At this point the 51st captured six pieces of artillery.

"The second day's battle, the 51st Indiana was the rear line of

the Brigade. In the afternoon, General Thomas J. Wood, commanding the Fourth Army Corps, rode up to General Beatty, then commanding the 3rd Division (Wood's old division) and ordered him
to mass his division, charge and carry the Overton Hills at all
hazards. The division was massed in nine lines of battle—the 51st
Indiana being the 6th line—five lines in its front and three lines in
the rear. The charge was ordered and away they went, but a most
murderous fire met them. The brigade commander of the brigade
in the advance (General Post), when within some 400 yards of the
enemy's works, was shot. His command thought him dead and his
men all lay down as one man. The two lines of Streight's Brigade,
in advance of the 51st Indiana, also lay down when they ran up to
the other prostrate lines. At that time young Anderson was left
solely in command of his regiment. He called to the officer in his
immediate front to ask why he was stopping, and why his men were
lying down instead of going on and up the hill. He was answered
that the men were lying down because those in front did.

" 'Why don't you order them up and onward?'

" 'I have, but they will not go.'

" 'Well, I can take *my* regiment on,' said Anderson. (He was then
just twenty-five years old and had 800 men under him with but
seven officers in the line; *three* companies were commanded by
their orderly sergeants.)

" 'Well, you can do more than I can with mine.'

"Sinking his spurs into his horse's sides, Anderson ran over the
five lines of battle in his front. He ordered his regiment to charge,
bayonets, double quick. This gallant old regiment, with some 400
veterans and 400 drafted men and substitutes, responded to the
command and without a waver in its line, without *one* single man
lying down, swept over the *five* other lines. On and on the brave
boys followed their intrepid and daring young commander, through
a murderous fire into the mouth of hell. The ranks were thinning,
but still up they go, following their leader. The works are being
forsaken; ten pieces of artillery in their immediate front are being
abandoned. The rebels are running; only a moment or two more
and they will be on the works. But, alas, when within thirty feet
of the works, and about 100 feet in front of his line, while riding at
full speed from the left toward the center and right, a sharpshooter
picked off this gallant young officer, and he fell in the edge of the

" 'He ordered his regiment to charge, bayonets, double quick.' "—*Wood engraving,* Harper's Weekly, *from a sketch by George H. Ellsbury, depicting the Battle of Nashville, fought on December 15 and 16, 1864*

(FORT WARD MUSEUM)

abatis, almost in the trenches of the enemy, pierced through the hip and spine. . . . His wound was pronounced mortal, and because the surgeons thought he would die he received no attention for over twenty-six hours. But, by the aid of his sound constitution and a good deal of grit, he pulled through. His recovery was remarkable, for he again took the field in the spring of '65."

I V

Boots and Saddles

THE greatest of all conflicts in the history of the United States has often been called the last war between gentlemen, and a great deal of its especial appeal stems from this concept of its nature.

In a very real way the cavalry epitomized the romantic dashing spirit of the times. Whenever the name Jeb Stuart is mentioned there springs to mind with very little effort a picture of a gay, chivalric cavalier wearing a magnificent gray uniform, a flowing cape, a swaying plume on his hat, accompanied by his banjo-strumming orderly, Corporal Sweeny, playing "Jine the Cavalry."

The first two years of the war were the best years for the southern cavalryman who, born and bred to the saddle, completely outclassed his northern opponent. Superbly mounted, possessed of supreme confidence in his ability, the cavalryman of the South rode rings around his frustrated, bewildered, suffering enemy. Here and there, more often in the divided state of Kentucky, where the armies of both sides contained numbers of gifted horsemen, there were times when the northern cavalry appeared to good advantage but, for the most part, the victories time and again were won by the bold horsemen of the Confederacy. As long as the southern cavalryman could continue to obtain a good mount, and necessary forage for it, his superiority went unchallenged. But as the Confederate armies ran short of supplies the first to feel the pinch were the mounted forces. Because the shortages included both food and forage the cavalry felt these shortages far more keenly than the infantry. Superb horsemen though they were, trained by years of experience in how to care for their mounts, officers and men alike discovered that they were facing an insoluble problem when it came to fighting a war with weakened, undernourished animals for whom they could obtain not even the minimum supplies required.

Again and again, more and more often, they found themselves without any horses at all.

The history of cavalry warfare in this great conflict between the North and South is a true index of the way the entire war went. In the beginning it appeared as if the North would be forced to let the southern states go free. Thereafter the pendulum swung slowly and inexorably in the opposite direction. Northern cavalrymen finally began to learn the rudiments of horsemanship, the care and feeding of their mounts, and though still individually outclassed in the skills of a cavalryman, their mass more than made up for individual deficiencies. The northern cavalry had no supply problems. Horses, food, and forage were available in more than sufficient quantity. With greatly superior numbers, far better equipped, superbly armed, in many cases with the new repeating carbines, the northern cavalry were easily able to overrun and crush their opponents almost by sheer weight of numbers and firepower.

Simultaneously the character of the war itself was changing. To a great extent it had lost its gentlemanly flavor. Major General Philip H. Sheridan made a name for himself by devastating and plundering the once fertile Shenandoah Valley. Yet, in spite of the changed character of the war, symbolized by the smoke, burning, and ruthless destruction wrought by Sheridan, the cavalry arm of the service never wholly lost its glamourous appeal for the men of either side. Throughout the four years of warfare they considered themselves the élite of the Army and proudly wore their spurs to proclaim their superiority.

It may be expected that in such a group there would be some who were not overmodest about their achievements. Such a one was Julius D. Rhodes who wrote of his own exploits: "His last action cannot find a superior in any army."

Rhodes's penmanship was outstandingly graceful, flowing, even elegant in style. He closed one of his letters with the words:
"I am Fraternally Yours,
in F C & L"
a reference to the Grand Army of the Republic motto of "Friendship, Charity and Loyalty." Many of the veterans used this same complimentary close indicating membership in the organization.

Julius D. Rhodes was cited for bravery at Thoroughfare Gap on

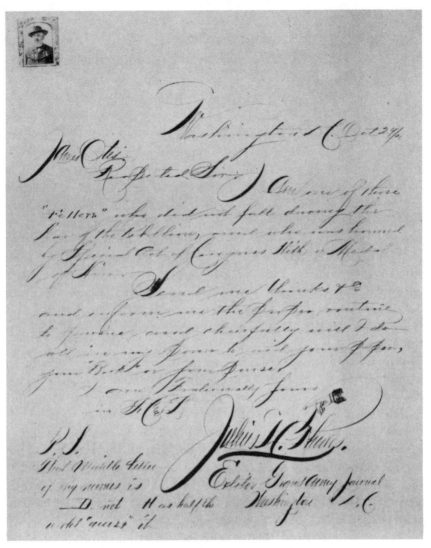

"Rhodes's penmanship was outstandingly graceful . . ."

August 28, 1862, and at Bull Run on August 30, but his letter was by no means confined to his activities on those two days.

"Julius Dexter Rhodes was born in the City of Monroe, Michigan, October 1, 1841. At the age of seven, his parents moved to Springville, Erie County, New York, where he was raised and educated at Springville Institute. At the first call to arms, he enlisted in the 21st New York Infantry, but his parents would not consent to his entering the service. At the second call for troops he was the first man to enlist in his town for the cavalry arm of the service, which was on September 3, 1861.

"His first smell of burnt powder was at Harrisonburg, Virginia, May 6, 1862 when he was acting bugler. A charge was ordered by Major Vought who was in charge of a detachment of the 5th New York Cavalry. As soon as the charge was sounded and Ashby's forces put to flight, Major Vought rode up to Julius D. Rhodes, and ordered him to sound a retreat. Rhodes, seeing the enemy broken and put to flight, and thinking the major had made a mistake in giving his order, re-sounded the charge, which resulted in a complete victory for the Union forces. . . . One Union soldier was killed (a bugler), and the adjutant was taken prisoner. The Confederates lost 7 killed and 3 taken prisoner. Rhodes was reduced to the ranks that night for sounding a charge when a retreat had been ordered.

"We next find him at Waterloo Bridge, Virginia. When 10 volunteers were called to burn the bridge under the guns of two Confederate regiments, Rhodes was the first volunteer to tender his services and, out of the 10 volunteers, every one was either hit or wounded with the exception of Rhodes, who escaped untouched. His action in this affair caused much comment. One of the 10 men, who was carrying a bottle of turpentine with which to ignite the bridge, was severely wounded, which caused him to fall and drop the bottle of turpentine. Rhodes ran back, picked up the decanter of fluid, ran to the center of the bridge, and broke the bottle of turpentine upon the bundles of wood prepared to fire the bridge; the structure was destroyed and the cavalry carried out their purpose.

"Rhodes was shortly afterwards detached from his regiment on special duty as a scout for General John Buford of cavalry fame, where he distinguished himself in the presence of Buford and the officers of his staff. Three Confederates were endeavoring to escape across an open field when Rhodes asked the general the privilege of capturing them, which was promptly given by the general. In less time than it would take to narrate it, one was killed, and the other two brought in by Rhodes and turned over to General Buford. It was a clear capture for, after turning the prisoners over to the general, Rhodes' horse fell dead, having been shot through by the Confederate who was killed by Rhodes for firing upon him.

"After two long nights' travel, being compelled to take to the woods to evade capture, we find him connected with the 105th

New York Infantry Volunteers. . . . This regiment was engaged at Thoroughfare Gap with the advance of Longstreet's Confederate forces. A skirmish line was called for. Rhodes stepped up to the lieutenant colonel commanding and made the following remark: 'Colonel, give me a musket and I will lead your skirmish line.' A musket was given him by Sergeant A. J. Longmode and Rhodes led the line with such determination that his actions were the comment of all the officers and men. Two days later he performed the same hazardous duties at Bull Run, August 30, 1862, and, while leading the skirmish line and far in advance of the skirmishers, he was the first man to scale the railroad grade, and the first one to fall, shot in two places. He was left where he fell, and supposed killed. But he managed to use a gun for a crutch, escaped capture, and was taken to Harewood Hospital, Washington, D.C., where he was discharged on February 27, 1863.

"We next find him in New Orleans, Louisiana, where he went to care for his only brother, Julian H. Rhodes, of Company F, 116th New York Volunteers. He had been there but a few days when he tendered his services to General Banks to lead one of the companies in the 'Forlorn Hope' at Port Hudson. Owing to the capitulation of Port Hudson on July 9, the storming brigade was not called upon to assault the works, but the honor falls with as much credit to the brave men as though they had lost their lives.

"At the Battle of Donaldsville, Louisiana, Rhodes was lying under an orange tree suffering with typhus fever. But as soon as the booming of cannon broke upon his ear, he mounted his horse and in a few moments was engaged in the battle beside his brother. His action in this engagement was spoken of in the general report of the battle.

"His last action cannot find a superior in any army. He was a sergeant in Company M, 31st Maine Volunteers. On the morning of April 2, 1865, while his regiment was leading the charge upon Petersburg, Virginia, the first assault was made upon Fort Mahone. Rhodes, while scaling the ramparts, was knocked down three times by the butt of a musket, his skull being broken 3 inches in length. He was pierced through the cheek with a bayonet. He killed the Confederate who pierced him with a sergeant's sword, and was the 2nd man over the enemy's works. His head was bandaged with a handkerchief and he led his company with desperate bravery as there was no officer in command of the company. Three other forts were assaulted by his command and, in each assault, he proved himself with such determined bravery that General Parke's Chief of Staff asked his name, company and regiment in the heat of the battle. He became unconscious at 3:30 p.m., was that night sent to the hospital, and discharged at Augusta, Maine, on October 18, 1865. He is living today in Washington, D.C. and is a true friend to all old comrades, and a very popular lecturer upon the battles of the Rebellion."

The method that Joel H. Lyman of Randolph, New York, adopted to tell his story of winning the Medal of Honor was to find someone else to describe the circumstances for him. The man he chose was William G. Hills, "another 'Medal Man' who was awarded the medal for helping me off the field on the 26th of September, 1864, which will give you an idea as to the granting of the medal."

Ex-Quartermaster Sergeant Lyman asked for a copy of the book when it was completed and was very careful to furnish accurate information concerning his record of service. "I send you by mail the proceedings of the reunion of my regiment, which contains the battles. You will see many of them checked. Those so checked I was *not* in. After the fight at Meadow Bridge I was detailed to accompany the wounded to Point Lookout General Hospital."

It is most fortunate, as well as appropriate, that Private Hills was selected to describe the battles because the story of how he won his medal is also told. The actions described were, in every way, more typical of the mounted cavalry charges that recruits envisioned when they first enlisted in the cavalry.

"My name is William G. Hills. I reside in St. Louis, Missouri. I make the following sworn statement: I was a member of Company E, 9th New York Cavalry from its organization in October 1861 until mustered out of service October 1864. I was with my company and regiment on the 19th day of September, 1864, and was in the engagement that day on the Opequon Creek near Winchester. I never saw more gallantry displayed than that of the officers and men of the 9th New York Cavalry on that occasion. It was one succession of charges, first against cavalry, then against infantry and artillery, and from victory to victory.

"I saw the capture of the Confederate flag in our front, as men-

tioned in the statement of Captain Smith, and I distinctly remember when we (our regiment) met the charge of the Rebel cavalry, and charged them in turn; their ranks were completely broken, and their officers were making desperate efforts to rally their men around this flag, while their artillery was sweeping with shot and shell every part of the ground we occupied; our bugles were sounding the rally for the regiment to reform. It was at this time that I saw Sergeant J. H. Lyman and Lieutenant Smith make a dash in the direction of the Rebel flag. They were riding close together when Lieutenant Smith's horse was shot and fell, and, as it appeared, very nearly unhorsed Sergeant Lyman, who soon recovered and pushed on for the flag, which had been secured by another party who was favored by the accident which delayed Lyman, who though failing to secure the trophy he was after, did not return without a prize, for he brought back with him a Confederate line officer, whom he disarmed in my immediate presence as my company was forming its line.

"The desperate attempt of Sergeant Lyman to capture the flag on that occasion, and the successful capture of a Confederate officer,

as well armed as himself, was a gallant act; and won for him the esteem of the whole regiment; and I doubt if there is anyone now living, who was present on that occasion, who could not recall the gallant conduct of Sergeant Lyman at the Battle of Winchester.

"On the 26th day of September, 1864, I was with my regiment. We were engaged early in the day, and drove the enemy's cavalry across the north fork of the Shenandoah River near Port Republic, Virginia. Just as we reached the river a troop of the enemy's rear guard made a break for the ford, which was in our immediate front. I saw Sergeant J. H. Lyman ride rapidly down the slope toward the river as if to intercept the retreating enemy; he was entirely alone, and seemingly unconscious of the danger he was in, and was making good use of his carbine. General Early's whole army lay parked on the plain between the river and the mountains beyond, with a long line of infantry that patrolled the river, and in easy musket range of our advance, while along the opposite bank among the heavy growth of willows they had their rifle pits from which they opened on us, as well as from the line of infantry, a terrific fire. Sergeant Lyman was shot, and fell from his horse severely wounded, and our line was ordered to fall back. Inspired by a sense of duty I owed to one so brave, I went to his rescue, and took him to the rear amid a perfect shower of bullets.

"I am glad to add this statement of facts to those of his company commander, Captain Smith, sincerely believing that no more gallant soldier ever wore a medal than Joel H. Lyman."

Another former soldier who wanted a copy of the book ("Please let me know when the volume is ready for sale. I want it.") was Michael Sowers, born in Allegheny County, enlisted at Pittsburgh, Pennsylvania, in March 1864 as a private in Company L, 4th Pennsylvania Volunteer Cavalry. He also had a friend write his account for him.

" 'Little Mike,' as he was familiarly called, never shirked a dangerous duty. But with evident pride, often verging upon audacity, he set about its performance in a manner which at once reassured his comrades and elicited the warm approval of his officers.

"The 'Congressional Medal of Honor' was awarded him for distinguished bravery at the Battle of Stony Creek Station, Virginia, on December 1, 1864.

"Stony Creek is a branch of the Nottaway River and the station which bears its name was situated on the south bank of that stream at a point 20 miles south of Petersburg, where it is crossed by the Weldon Railroad. To this point the Confederates shipped the rich products of bread stuffs from the Roanoke Valley, carried them thence by wagons to the South Side Railroad, over which they reached Lee's hungry armies about Petersburg and Richmond.

"A well-garrisoned fort with artillery in positions, and well-manned, was situated on the south bank of the stream. Back of that were more houses filled with much needed supplies for Lee. Sowers' regiment was in the advance and charged mounted to the north bank of the creek opposite the fort. Finding the stream there impassable, it veered to its left, following the stream about ½ mile to a ford, where, under a heavy artillery fire, it crossed and came up in the rear of the fort and buildings. When within short musket range of the fort its progress was again checked by a deep and broad ditch or moat partly filled with brush and water. A point was soon found where a crossing was made by single or double file. All this time the regiment was under a destructive fire, and, as Sowers

"'Sowers' regiment was in the advance and charged mounted . . .'"
—*Pencil drawing by Alfred R. Waud, depicting a cavalry charge against earthworks*

crossed the ditch, his horse was shot and he found himself within the moat dismounted. Instead of seeking safety in the rear, he grasped his carbine; in a shower of bullets, on foot, and in advance of the mounted men who were still crossing the ditch, he made straight for the fort. He reached a pile of hay bales a few rods distant from the fort unharmed and, taking refuge behind them, opened fire on the enemy with his repeating carbine. Soon the charging column came up and, as the order to dismount was given for the purpose of scaling the fort, a white flag was displayed by the enemy. The brief but bloody battle was ended.

"Sowers now renewed his onward movement and was amongst the first of our men to enter the fort. The commandant, a major, had within the fort a fine horse. Sowers, seeking to replace his lost mount, seized the reins of the major's animal, informing that officer that he would take charge of the horse, as the major would have no further use for him. Here 'Little Mike' committed a pardonable unmilitary error for, instead of disarming the major, he demanded his canteen. While sampling its contents, the officer drew a revolver and shot the animal, leaving 'Little Mike' without a mount for the second time that day."

Sowers' letter-writing friend, telling the story from "Little Mike's" point of view, saw the humor in the situation. He labeled this momentary lapse as "a pardonable unmilitary error." The Confederate major, with a more realistic sense of values forced upon him by the necessity of fighting a war against greatly superior numbers, would probably have reversed the wording and called it "an unpardonable military error." Here were representatives of two completely opposite systems. Sowers' horse had been furnished him by the United States government; Confederate officers and men generally had to supply their own horses, at their expense. The major could have seen very little humor in the situation. How deeply it must have hurt to offer this sacrifice to military necessity, to shoot and kill his favorite horse to prevent it from falling into the hands of the enemy.

All true cavalrymen, no matter what their origin, have a common bond in their love for horses. That one of their number could have won the Congressional Medal of Honor astride a mule is almost inconceivable, but it happened.

The soldier who performed this remarkable feat was a young man from Ohiopyle, Fayette County, Pennsylvania, named Francis Marion Cunningham. It was almost inevitable that anyone named for that illustrious South Carolina patriot, Francis Marion (The Swamp Fox), would have joined the cavalry. In early April 1865 Cunningham was on his second enlistment, serving as a sergeant in Company H of the 1st West Virginia Cavalry.

At first he was reluctant to write about his wartime service, not because it involved a mule, but because he did not wish to speak or write about himself. His explanatory letter has already been quoted.

Francis M. Cunningham paid a very high tribute to the courage and strong sense of duty of his opponents at Sayler's Creek when he called it "one of the hardest cavalry fights of the war." It is doubtful that he realized just how high a tribute he was paying. Those who faced him on that day had been on near-starvation rations for months on end, yet were unhesitatingly offering themselves as sacrifices in order that the remainder of the Confederate army might escape to continue the retreat which would finally end three days later at Appomattox.

"The Battle of Sayler's Creek, on April 6, 1865, I regarded as one of the hardest cavalry fights of the war.

"I had the honor of belonging to Custer's 3rd Cavalry Division, my regiment being the 1st West Virginia Cavalry. During the afternoon we had made a number of charges, some of which were repulsed with severe loss of men and horses. I had two horses killed under me. In the last charge of the day I rode a fine, fleet footed mule, which was also badly wounded. The last charge was the one that broke Ewell's lines. This charge I led with but three men left of my company to follow me. We were charging a line of infantry behind a fence. The mule jumped the fence carrying me in among the Rebels where they were pretty thick. I had some lively work on hand, and a good deal of trouble with about three of the Rebel color guard before I got within striking distance of the colors of the 12th Virginia Infantry. I then had a lively set-to with the color bearer. The poor fellow fought bravely for his colors but the mule and I were too much for him. . . .

"I was sent with a few of my comrades direct to Washington in charge of Colonel Sherman, with a recommendation from General Sheridan as being worthy of any favor that the government might see proper to bestow upon us. We were presented in a body to Stanton, the Secretary of War. He received us in the presence of a lot of distinguished generals, statesmen, governors, etc. Quite a display was made over us; all received Medals of Honor. I afterwards received a Medal of Honor from the state, or rather from the governor of West Virginia.

"The above is a brief sketch of how I won the medals. I have never given out any statement of the facts to anyone for publication and only do so now because my children have been teasing me to do it. I served four years in the army, participated in 74 battles and skirmishes, was slightly wounded four times.

"During the war I was possessed of wonderful strength and endurance. I am now badly used up. But my greatest of all earthly desires is to see my country prosperous and happy.

"God bless you My Comrade

"God bless our Country."

V

Forward the Guns

PRIOR to the seventeenth century the artillery gunner was a specialist practicing an art or science whose trade secrets he jealously guarded. Guns were usually heavy and cumbersome, useful only for siege warfare, and supposedly only an expert was qualified to use one of these mysterious things. As a result artillery of that period played only a very minor role on the battlefield. A few farsighted individuals had introduced light cannon hauled by horses to keep pace with the infantry but these were so few in number that they were regarded as novelties rather than as forerunners of the future. Battles were won by either infantry or cavalry.

By the nineteenth century all this had been changed radically. Three individuals had been primarily responsible. Gustavus Adolphus, the great King of Sweden, who may justly be termed the founder of modern tactics and warfare, had seen the need for light mobile guns. During the Thirty Years' War in Germany (1618–48), he had introduced field artillery in quantity and combined the actions of the three arms: infantry, cavalry, and artillery. Henceforth no army could afford to wage war without cannon capable of being brought into action on the battlefield.

In the eighteenth century a Frenchman, Jean Baptiste de Gribeauval, introduced reforms and reorganizations in France that made the French artillery famous throughout the world. He provided distinct matériel for field, siege, garrison, and sea-coast use. Field batteries were limited in size; guns were reduced in length and weight, and profuse ornamentation discarded. Carriages were strengthened with iron axletrees. Everything was made light, uniform, and interchangeable. Horses were harnessed in pairs instead of in tandem; batteries came into action at a gallop. Gribeauval may accurately be called the father of modern field artillery.

Then came the greatest artilleryman of all, Napoleon Bonaparte, who taught all armies how field artillery should be used. From that time forward the role of artillery became increasingly more decisive until, in World War I, 75 to 80 per cent of the casualties inflicted in battle were caused by artillery.

During the Civil War proper or improper use of field artillery, by one side or the other, on several occasions spelled the difference between victory or defeat. When the command, "Forward the Guns. Bring the Artillery Forward," echoed over a battlefield it was almost invariably a sign of impending victory, for the guns accompanied the attacking waves of infantry to fight beside them in the front line.

On occasion, however, batteries were brought forward prematurely to find themselves caught in a counterattack, the target for the combined fire of the enemy's infantry as well as the enemy's artillery. In the very first large battle of the war at Bull Run, near Manassas, Virginia, this occurred. Two U.S. artillery batteries were hurried forward to an exposed position, supported by the New York Fire Zouave regiment and a battalion of marines, where they immediately became engaged with the Confederate artillery. A cavalry charge, led by Colonel J. E. B. Stuart, scattered the supporting troops. The 33rd Virginia of Jackson's brigade (which here acquired the name Stonewall Brigade) advanced. In the confusion of the moment it was thought to be friendly.

Thirty-three years after the event an officer of one of the two batteries was asked to tell the story of how he, as a lieutenant, had won the Medal of Honor on that memorable day. A lot of water had passed under the bridge in the intervening years but Adelbert Ames, writing from Lowell, Massachusetts, made no mention of any of it. On the form provided, he recorded that he had been born in Rockland (then East Thomaston), Maine, and had been graduated from West Point in the Class of May 1861, just two months before the First Battle of Bull Run. Of his subsequent life he said nothing, although he had risen to the rank of major general, had been appointed military governor of Mississippi, married Benjamin F. "Beast" Butler's only daughter, served as a United States senator and then as governor of Mississippi in the carpetbag period.

Adelbert Ames was equally noncommittal about his winning of the medal: " 'The story of how I won the Medal' is all found in my Captain's report; and is no doubt all you want." Fortunately Captain, later Major General, Charles Griffin's official report is far more graphic.

"The battery opened upon the enemy's battery amidst a galling fire from his artillery, and continued firing for near half an hour. It then changed position to the right and fired two rounds, when it was charged by the enemy's infantry from the woods on the right of our position. This infantry was mistaken for our own forces, an officer on the field having stated that it was a regiment sent by Colonel Heintzelman to support the battery. In this charge of the enemy every cannoneer was cut down and a large number of horses killed, leaving the battery (which was without support except in name) perfectly helpless. Owing to the loss of men and horses, it was impossible to take more than three pieces from the field. Two of these were afterwards lost in the retreat, by the blocking up of the road by our own forces and the complete exhaustion of the few horses dragging them. The same thing happened with reference to the battery wagon, forge, and one caisson. All that is left of the battery is one Parrott rifle gun and one 12-pounder howitzer limber.

"Of the 95 men who went into action 27 are killed, wounded, and missing, and of 101 horses 55 are missing.

"In conclusion, I would state that my officers and men behaved in a most gallant manner, displaying great fearlessness, and doing their duty as becomes brave soldiers.

"P.S. In addition, I deem it my duty to add that Lieutenant Ames was wounded so as to be unable to ride on a horse at almost the first fire; yet he sat by his command directing the fire, being helped on and off the caisson during the different changes of front or position, refusing to leave the field until he became too weak to sit up."

An artillery battery posted to defend a vital point in the front lines would automatically draw attention upon itself. The enemy artillery would be sure to concentrate its fire upon that battery in preparation for an infantry assault. If badly outnumbered gun for gun, or if caught without any warning by a sudden blast of concentrated gunfire at short range, the defenders would stand little chance of survival.

Former private John F. Chase of Augusta, Maine, gave a vivid description of what happened to the 5th Battery, Maine Light

Artillery, on the third day of the great Battle of Chancellorsville, May 3, 1863.

"My battery, the 5th Maine, Captain George F. Leppien commanding, went into action at Chancellorsville, Sunday morning, May 3, 1863. Our position was at the right of the Chancellorsville House, with room for only our battery between the house and the woods.

"The enemy opened upon us with a masked battery at short range. The air was full of flying missiles of death. It did not seem as if a bird could live, and there was no chance for a man. But the men of the battery stood at their posts like the heroes they were.

"Our comrades were falling on all sides . . . our officers were either killed or wounded. What men there were left stood firm at their guns, pouring death and destruction into the advancing ranks of the enemy, charging across the plain to capture our guns.

"I was No. 1 cannoneer of the 6th gun. My duty was to ram cartridges. I soon stood alone at my gun; the crew had melted away, either killed or wounded. I went to the next gun and, in a few minutes, they all were gone. I then went to the third gun and in a short time there were only two of us left, Corporal Lebroke and myself. We fired the gun several times alone, until one of the enemy's shots struck our gun in the muzzle and battered it so we could not get a shot into it. At that moment Colonel Mulholland charged up with part of the Irish Brigade to save our guns. Comrade Lebroke and myself held up the trail of our gun while some of the 116th Pennsylvania and 28th Massachusetts helped draw it off the field.

"After our gun was safe from capture, I went back onto the field after Lieutenant Kirby, an officer of the Regular Army, who had been sent in to take charge of our battery after our officers were all gone. His leg had been shattered as soon as he got onto the field, but he would not be taken off until the guns were safe. *He was a hero.*

"While I was carrying him off the field, he took Comrade Lebroke's and my name, and told me that if ever two men earned a Medal of Honor we had, and he would see that we got one. He died before he reached Washington but, like a true soldier, he made his report in the ambulance and that report is on file at the War Department.

"The reason I did not receive my medal at the time was that

" 'My battery, the 5th Maine, Captain George F. Leppien commanding,
—Etching "Going into Action" by W. H. Shelton, 1887

the next battle I went into was Gettysburg. I was so badly wounded that I was reported killed, losing an arm and an eye, and receiving 48 other wounds. After I got better I never made any claim for my medal, supposing that Lieutenant Kirby did not make any report, as he died soon after receiving his wounds. So my medal laid in the War Department for 23 years before I received it. But summing the matter all up, I only did my duty as the rest of my comrades did."

There were two kinds of light field artillery. The more common was horse-drawn artillery designed to accompany infantry on the march. In this type the cannoneers either walked or rode the cais-

went into action at Chancellorsville, Sunday morning, May 3, 1863.'"

sons and limbers, and frequently were called upon to help push the guns up hills.

The second type of light artillery was horse artillery. The difference was that every man was assigned a horse to ride. Its function was to accompany, and fight beside, the faster-moving cavalry.

Whenever horse artillery is mentioned one name immediately springs to mind—John Pelham of Alabama, the commander of Jeb Stuart's horse artillery. He had attended West Point (in the same class with Adelbert Ames) but, when his state seceded from the Union, he left the Academy to fight for the South. Although Major Pelham lived less than two years after the war began, he was universally known to the people of both the South and the North as "the gallant Pelham."

" 'Comrade Lebroke and myself held
up the trail of our gun while some
of the 116th Pennsylvania and 28th
Massachusetts helped draw it off the
field.' "—Wood engraving inspired by
the bravery shown on this occasion, from
Official and Illustrated War Record,
written and edited by General
Marcus J. Wright
(FORT WARD MUSEUM)

"Whenever horse artillery is mentioned
one name immediately springs to mind—
John Pelham of Alabama, the
commander of Jeb Stuart's horse
artillery."
(COOK COLLECTION, VALENTINE MUSEUM,
RICHMOND, VIRGINIA)

Of all the daring exploits for which John Pelham became so famous, the best known was his stirring action at the beginning of the Battle of Fredericksburg. With just two guns he galloped forward far in front of the Confederate lines, went into position on the flank of thousands of advancing northern troops and opened fire upon the startled enemy. One of his guns was soon disabled but with the other he fought four Union batteries, and halted the entire attack for the space of over half an hour, not returning to his lines until his ammunition was almost gone.

The Battle of Fredericksburg, fought on December 13, 1862, was a clear-cut Confederate victory; not so Trevilian Station, a two-day battle fought on June 11–12, 1864. There were two divisions of cavalry engaged on each side, commanded by General Philip H. Sheridan and General Wade Hampton respectively. Each claimed victory but Hampton's claim seems much more justified.

In a battle of cavalry against cavalry, the two field artillerymen whose accounts are given here were both therefore serving with horse artillery batteries. The action stories of these two men, both of whom were in the Regular Army for well over thirty years, have some points of similarity but they end quite differently.

When the war began, Edward B. Williston was living in San Francisco, California, but he was a Vermonter, born in Norwich, a graduate of Norwich University. So he came back East to take part in the struggle for the Union. He arrived too late to take part in the First Battle of Bull Run but participated in every other major battle fought by the Army of the Potomac beginning with the Second Battle of Bull Run.

Now, thirty-three years later, Major Williston had been asked to furnish information about his Medal of Honor award. From the Office of the Inspector of Artillery, Headquarters, Department of the Missouri, he sent two pieces of paper. The first was the recommendation his brigade commander, Brigadier General Wesley Merritt, had sent to the Adjutant General of the Army; the second was an extract from General Merritt's official report of the Battle of Trevilian Station. Together they told the story.

Major Williston's letter, the questionnaire that he completed showing his wartime service and the battles in which he participated, and the other papers that he sent to James Otis were presented to President Harry S Truman by Charlie Kohen, who remembered the President's statement that he would rather have won the medal than be President of the United States.

In order to give the President a choice, Kohen appeared with a group of twenty-one letters from his collection. While President Truman and his military aide, Major General Harry H. Vaughan, were studying the letters, General Vaughan suddenly exclaimed: "Eureka! Here it is!" The reason this letter was selected is obvious. Edward B. Williston was an artillery officer who, like Harry S Truman in World War I, commanded a Battery D in combat.

"I have the honor to recommend that Major E. B. Williston, 3rd U.S. Artillery, be awarded, under A. R. 175, a Medal of Honor for having especially distinguished himself at the action of Trevilian Station, Virginia, June 12, 1864. Major Williston, then a lieutenant, was in command of Horse Battery D, 2nd U.S. Artillery. In the

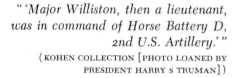

" 'Major Williston, then a lieutenant, was in command of Horse Battery D, 2nd U.S. Artillery.' "
(KOHEN COLLECTION [PHOTO LOANED BY PRESIDENT HARRY S TRUMAN])

crisis of the action at Trevilian, when my lines were being pressed by an overwhelming force of the enemy, Lieutenant Williston planted three guns of his battery in an exposed but favorable position for effective work; and then personally moved the fourth gun onto the skirmish line. Using double charges of canister he, by his individual efforts, greatly aided in resisting successfully the charges of the enemy on our front. The loss of the brigade, reduced at that time in strength, was twelve (12) officers killed and wounded and two hundred and twenty-two (222) men."

In his official report of the action General Merritt waxed considerably more eloquent.

"Right gallantly did the battery come up in the midst of a heavy musketry fire, we being at that time so close to the enemy that their shells all flew far over us. Planting three guns of the battery in this position, where it dealt the enemy heavy blows, Lieutenant Williston moved one of his brass 12-pounders onto the skirmish line. In fact, the line was moved to the front to allow him to get an eligible position, where he remained with his gun, in the face of the strengthened enemy (who advanced to its very muzzle), dealing death and destruction in their ranks with double loads of canister."

When Lieutenant Williston and his gun crew moved their lone gun up in advance of the others, in front of the main line up with the skirmishers, they voluntarily placed themselves in a very perilous position in order to fire more effectively upon the advancing enemy. Lest there be any doubt as to the risks they ran, listen to the story of what happened to another lone gun exposed in a similar way at Trevilian Station on the preceding day.

The hero of this action was a soldier who, when Fort Sumter was fired upon in April 1861, had already served nearly three and one-half years of a five-year enlistment. John Kennedy was born in Cavan, Ireland, on May 14, 1834. The records describe him as being five feet, seven and one-half inches tall, having red hair, blue eyes, and a ruddy complexion. It is apparent that the Kennedy family was among the many thousands who came to this country as a result of the great potato famine in Ireland and, following in the footsteps of many another Irishman who found work hard to get in the late 1850's, Kennedy had enlisted in the army.

Prior to the Civil War, his army career appears to have been fairly uneventful, although he recorded that he had been with Battery M of the 2nd U.S. Artillery on the Utah expedition of 1858. During the war, however, he had fought with his battery on many hotly contested fields. By the time of the Battle of Trevilian Station he was on his second enlistment; eventually he would serve seven enlistments and retire as an ordnance sergeant after thirty-three years of honorable service.

The first document that John Kennedy submitted was a recommendation sent to the Adjutant General by Captain Carle A. Woodruff, a man who certainly should have known about Medal of Honor awards because he himself was a recipient for saving his guns from an attack by Confederate infantry in July 1863.

"Twenty-eight years ago today, at the Battle of Trevilian Station, Virginia, June 11, 1864, an act of conspicuous bravery came to my notice which I think has never had mention, viz:—one gun of Lieutenant William Egan's section of Horse Battery M, 2nd Artillery was placed in a somewhat dangerous position. Almost immediately after reaching said position, the piece was charged by the Confederate cavalry and, so impetuous was the charge, that but one round could be fired. Failing to check the cavalry, and fearing the capture of his men, Lieutenant Egan ordered them to retreat. The limber had already been withdrawn, making it impossible to carry off the piece if captured. The Gunner Corporal, John Kennedy, now Ordnance Sergeant (retired), and Private Charles O'Neil remained at the gun. Kennedy used his handspike and O'Neil, who was No. 1, used the sponge staff upon the advancing foe, but both were captured and taken to Andersonville where O'Neil died."

This official statement is fairly descriptive but John Kennedy's own personal recital makes better reading. He wrote that he was awarded the Medal of Honor "for the Battle of Trevilian Station, June 11, 1864. The battery was with Custer's cavalry brigade. The brigade was detached from Sheridan's command of two divisions . . . to strike this station early in the morning of June 11, '64. We attacked Fitzhugh Lee's and Wade Hampton's Cavalry Divisions, and kept up the unequal contest until General Sheridan could come 4 miles to our assistance.

"Well, by the time General Sheridan came on the scene, things looked blue, the battery losing 4 caissons with their horses, harness and contents. The gun, a 12-pound brass, which I was gunner of, was detached a little ways in front of the rifle platoons. Well, a little before relief came, they charged the gun. In the confusion the limber managed to escape, leaving me and 4 men at the gun. With our ammunition gone, in the tussle, we used our pistols.

"When we emptied them we took the sponge staves and handspikes and used them freely until overpowered, by their actually riding us down. I was fencing with the handspike with a cavalry-

*" 'The gun, a 12-pound brass, which I was gunner of, was detached a
little ways in front of the rifle platoons.' "*

man when another came in rear of me and knocked me down, and
they then took us prisoner."

There followed a list of seven prisons in which he had been confined before the war had ended.

It seems most appropriate to quote his final letter to the Adjutant General.

"Little Rock Arkansas
August 23d 1892.

To The.
Adjutant General U.S. Army
Washington, D.C.

Sir

I have the honor to acknowledge receipt of Medal of Honor on
22d Inst. and for which I am very thankful to the United States and

their Officers concerned on behalf of your humble servant who always tried to the best of my ability to do my duty, and I also thank the Adjutant of the Army for his assistance in the matter.

Very respectfully your Obedient Servant
John Kennedy
Ord. Sergt. Ret.[a]
1308 Welsh St
Little Rock
Arks."

V I

On Seas and Rivers

"I HAVE noticed, or rather have failed to notice, since 1865, any particular attention paid to the common seaman, or man-o-war's man who so valiantly fought from '61 to '65.

"I served in one capacity or another in the U.S. Navy from '63 to '68 and have been so favorably impressed with the magnitude of the services rendered by the Navy in crushing the Rebellion; and which I contend would have never been crushed without their co-operation; that it seems to me strange that we hear or see so little about the work and heroism of the seaman, on river, gulf or ocean."

Writing from De Witt, Nebraska, in 1890, Dr. James K. L. Duncan felt thoroughly justified in making these complaints. Just the year before, he had purchased a book purporting to tell of the heroic achievements of servicemen during the Civil War but had failed "to find any heroism mentioned regarding a Sailor Boy." To a former sailor who had served on a "tinclad" on the Mississippi River, such shameful neglect of the Navy was inexcusable.

John G. Morrison, former coxswain, U.S.S. *Carondelet,* took a somewhat different attitude. "I did not intend to pay any attention to your letter, as I don't care a straw what posterity will or may think of me or my career, but I concluded to answer you as I thought common decency required that at my hands. A photograph I cannot send as I never had one taken in my life. I have an ambrotype taken in '62, and that is all."

This Irish immigrant, who before the war was a storekeeper in Lansingburg, New York, continued: "Although I enlisted as a soldier I got my medal for service in the Navy. I was transferred from the Army (at my own request) to the Navy, February 17, 1862. I was sent to the Western Flotilla under Foote and served on the gunboats *Carondelet* and *Lafayette* until my time was out, taking part in all the operations on the Mississippi, Yazoo, Red and other rivers. I reenlisted September 8, '64 in Company C, 21st New York Cavalry and served until May 28, '65. I send you a copy of the report for which I got the medal, the original being now on file in the Navy Department, Washington, D.C."

The act of heroism for which Morrison had been cited in general orders occurred on July 15, 1862. On that date the home-made Confederate ram *Arkansas,* built at Yazoo City, had steamed down the river to engage the Union fleet of nearly forty ships in the vicinity of Vicksburg. En route she was met by three gunboats, one of them the *Carondelet.* The result of the preliminary clash was predictable, although the sequel was not. Heavily outgunned, the three ships bravely met the Confederate ram and took a terrible beating. The sequel shows what little chance these three

"Heavily outgunned, the three ships bravely met the Confederate ram and took a terrible beating."—Wood engraving of the engagement between the Carondelet *and the* Arkansas, *from* Frank Leslie's Famous Leaders and Battle Scenes of the Civil War

(FORT WARD MUSEUM)

really had against this formidable opponent. For, with the odds then heavily against her, the ram smashed its way past the entire fleet and came to rest under the guns of Vicksburg.

For his part in the battle the Navy Department commended Coxswain Morrison for being the leader when boarders were called on deck, then the first to return to the guns to give the ram a broadside. "His presence of mind in time of battle or trial is reported as always conspicuous and encouraging."

Apparently it was not considered too unusual in those days to become associated first with the Army, then the Navy and return again to the Army. Franklin W. Lutes, writing from the town of Wolcott, New York, close by the shores of Lake Ontario, described a varied career ashore and afloat.

In 1861 he had "helped to recruit a company for the 9th Michigan Infantry, but did not go with that regiment. Shipped about this time in the *F. B. Bruce* as wheelsman. While in Buffalo, I shipped in the U.S. Navy in the gunboat *Michigan,* which was recruiting along the lakes. Was sent aboard the old receiving ship *North Carolina* which lay in the Brooklyn Navy Yard. I laid there from June until the last of August, or the first of September. Was then detailed aboard the sloop of war *Adirondack.* I do not remember the exact date when I went to sea. After cruising awhile, the first prize we captured was a schooner, the *Emma* of Nassau. She was laden with salt, flannels and shoes for the Southern Confederacy.

"I was detailed in another crew to fetch her into Philadelphia. After leaving the Navy, I went home to Michigan, was drafted in the 8th Michigan Cavalry, but would not go as a drafted man. Came to Clyde, Wayne County, New York, in March 1864. Enlisted in the 111th New York Volunteers."

Franklin Lutes's medal was awarded him, not by the Navy, but by the Army, for capturing a Confederate flag at Petersburg in March 1865.

In land warfare, cooperation and coordination between the various components of an army is of the utmost importance and may spell the difference between defeat and victory. In the navy, however, failure on the part of one individual may well mean the loss of an entire ship. Nor is it necessarily true that the most dangerous place in a battle is the most exposed position, on deck, or in the rigging. The sailors serving below may be running far greater risks in the performance of their assigned duties. The officers and men on the decks above can, at least, follow the progress of the battle, whereas the engineers, the firemen, and the other ratings stationed below often have no way of even guessing when disaster may strike.

One of the most hazardous operations that ships could undertake in the Civil War was to attempt, in the confined waters of a river channel, to pass shore batteries where guns had been placed in position, and sited in advance, for the express purpose of preventing passage at that point. And, if the move had to be made upstream, against the flow of the current, the danger was materially increased because the ships would remain exposed to the fire of the shore batteries for a greater length of time.

On March 14, 1863, Rear Admiral David G. Farragut's squadron of seven ships moved up the Mississippi River to attempt a passage of the strong Confederate batteries in position at Port Hudson, Louisiana. The squadron consisted of four heavy ships and three gunboats. The heavier ships, *Hartford, Richmond,* and *Monongahela* led the way, each with a gunboat lashed to it on the side away from the fort. Thus the larger ships protected the smaller. The U.S.S. *Mississippi* brought up the rear.

Of all the ships engaged, only the *Hartford* with the smaller *Albatross* weathered the storm of shot and shell from the batteries. The *Richmond* was hit in her steam plant, disabling her so that, even with the aid of the smaller *Genesee,* she could make no headway against the current, and was forced to turn back, suffering continuously from the fire of the shore batteries until she was out of range of the guns.

The *Monongahela* ran aground, took terrific punishment from the Port Hudson batteries, then was brought off with the help of the *Kineo* lashed alongside, and eventually also drifted downstream. The *Mississippi* also ran aground, but could not be refloated. Her crew was forced to abandon her. The shell bursts set the ship on fire and it exploded with a tremendous concussion.

In 1890, John Rush, of Washington, D.C., was asked to describe his part in this battle. He was careful to point out that he had not been the only one involved.

"I received your letter requesting information of my service

"On March 14, 1863, Rear Admiral David G. Farragut's squadron of seven ships moved up the Mississippi River to attempt a passage of the strong Confederate batteries in position at Port Hudson, Louisiana."—Painting by E. Packbauer

(LIBRARY OF CONGRESS)

rendered during the war. There were three men besides myself who got medals for the same act, the details of which I will send you in a few days. Their names are Joseph Vantine, Matthew McClelland, and John Hickman."

Fireman First Class John Rush wrote that he had been in the U.S. Navy for several years prior to the war and had taken part in all the engagements in which the *Richmond* had participated, from the beginning of the war to the date of his discharge.

"The following extract from papers awarding the medal will probably give better information of the service than if I recited same from memory. I can only say that it was the hottest half hour ever experienced by a human being who lived afterwards.

" 'The Medal of Honor was presented to John Rush, 1st Class Fireman for the following: United States Steamer *Richmond* in the attack on the Port Hudson batteries, March 14th, 1863; when the fire-room and other parts of the ship were filled with hot steam from injury to the boiler by a shot, these men from the first moment of the casualty, stood firmly at their posts, and were conspicuous in their exertions to remedy the evil, by hauling the fires from the injured boiler—the heat being so great from the combined effects of fire and steam, that they were compelled from mere exhaustion to relieve each other every few minutes until the work was accomplished.'

"I regret that I am unable to furnish the addresses of my comrades who received medals at the time I did. One of them I believe is dead and the other two, if I remember rightly, were residents of Philadelphia."

No book concerned with ships would be complete without at least one person in it who had run away to sea. The letter of a man named Jones was a little confusing, or was his name Martin? Eventually it became clear that he was one and the same person.

The official Navy Department record credits Edward S. Martin for performing his duties with skill and courage at the Battle of Mobile Bay on August 5, 1864, but the man who was awarded the medal was actually a bound apprentice named Edwin S. Jones. In order to get into the war, Jones had followed the time-honored, traditional pattern of running away and changing his name. It may be hopefully assumed that, when he returned a naval hero, his apprenticeship was forgotten, his future well assured.

Another sailor who was cited at Mobile Bay was Alexander Mack. The two men served in different ships, Jones as quartermaster of the U.S.S. *Galena*, Mack as captain of the Main Top, U.S.S. *Brooklyn,* but Alexander Mack had to intervene with the Navy medical authorities in order to assure his future.

The record says that: "Although wounded and sent below for treatment, Mack immediately returned to his post and took charge of his gun and, as heavy enemy return fire continued to fall, performed his duties with skill and courage until he was again wounded and totally disabled."

This was certainly not the end of the story as Alexander Mack recorded it: "The surgeon in Chelsea Hospital wanted to cut both legs off, the right one below the knee, the left below the hip—but I would not submit to it." The sailor's judgment proved to be better than the surgeon's. In 1872, Alexander Mack was appointed a boatswain in the U.S. Navy. Twenty-five years after the Battle of Mobile Bay, he was honorably retired on account of wounds and physical disability incurred in line of duty.

Of all the letters written to James Otis by personnel who served with the U.S. Navy during the Civil War, the longest and most informative came from a former orderly sergeant of the United States Marine Corps. This marine must have kept a diary. His letter comes pretty close to being a short history of the war at sea. In a postscript, John F. Mackie, who had joined the Corps at the Brooklyn Navy Yard in April 1861, added: "I have written fully so that you can strike out what is not necessary to a proper and interesting account."

Mackie also sent two appendices separately. These gave further details on his winning of the Medal of Honor and on the personal compliments he received from President Abraham Lincoln. For the sake of clarity, the contents of these appendices have been woven into the body of the letter. But these are the only changes that have been made, for it would be presumptuous indeed to delete any part of this record of service of the man who was the first member of the Marine Corps to be authorized a Congressional Medal of Honor.

"Was detailed as part of the Marine Guard of the U.S. Sloop of War *Savannah* about May 1, 1861 as a private of the Guard. The ship was ordered at once to Fortress Monroe, Virginia where we arrived shortly after the burning and destruction of the Norfolk Navy Yard. On June 10, 1861 the U.S.S. *Savannah* participated with other vessels in the attack upon Big Bethel. After this unfortunate affair we were ordered on blockade duty off the coast of North Carolina and assisted, with other ships, in the capture of Forts Hatteras and Clark, August 28 and 29, 1861, under Commodore Stringham.

"Returning again to Hampton Roads about the 1st of September 1861, U.S.S. *Savannah* took position up the James River as guard ship until the latter part of the month, during which time we were attacked several times by the rebel gunboats but received only trifling damage. We were relieved by the U.S.S. *Cumberland* and ordered to Port Royal, South Carolina.

"On the 7th of November, 1861, participated in the capture of Port Royal by Admiral S. F. DuPont. After the capture of the above place we were ordered, with other vessels, to assist in the capture of the islands and ports on the coast of Florida. The *Savannah* was ordered north about the 1st of January 1862 to New York City.

"March 1, 1862 was promoted corporal and ordered on board the U.S. Ironclad Ship *Galena*, Captain John Rodgers, and sailed in company with the U.S.S. *Monitor*, Captain Jno. L. Worden, for Fortress Monroe. During the passage we were delayed and did not arrive there until a few days after the destruction of the U.S. Ships *Congress* and *Cumberland* and the *Monitor's* famous battle with the rebel steamer *Merrimac*.

"April 1, 1862 we took an advanced position up the James River and on the 8th of May participated with other vessels in the attack and capture of Norfolk, the U.S. Navy Yard, and destroyed the rebel *Merrimac*. May 9th, we attacked the rebel batteries at Pigs Point and, after a hotly contested battle of four hours, captured both of the batteries, mounting 26 guns.[*]

"May 12, '62: Captured City Point after a short engagement during which the rebels set fire to the town, entirely destroying the place.

"May 15, 1862 attacked Fort Darling on the James River situated on Drewry's Bluff, below the City of Richmond. The fleet consisted of five vessels: *Galena, Monitor, Aroostook, Port Royal,* and *Naugatuck*.

"Captain John Rodgers anchored the *Galena*, 7 guns, in front of the fort about four hundred yards from the work. The other vessels were about eight hundred yards distant. Fort Darling is located on a bluff about one hundred feet above the river and mounted sixteen heavy guns in casemates; this elevation subjected the fleet to a plunging fire from the enemy's guns.

---

* On May 8, operations were begun against Norfolk. An unsuccessful attempt was made to lure the *Merrimac* out into deeper water. The city of Norfolk was actually captured on May 10. The Confederates evacuated the Navy Yard on the same date. The *Merrimac* was blown up by her crew to avoid capture on May 11. In the meantime the *Galena* had been sent upstream, at the personal suggestion of President Lincoln, to support General McClellan's army. This resulted in the attack and capture of the two batteries described by Mackie.

" ' . . . this elevation subjected the fleet to a plunging fire from the enemy's guns.' "—Rodgers' squadron engages Confederate batteries at Fort Darling, Drewry's Bluff, on the James River.

"At 6 o'clock a.m. the *Galena* opened fire on the fort. The enemy replied vigorously, killing and wounding several of our men before we got into position, Captain Rodgers being one of the first men wounded. From that time on until noon the *Galena* poured into the fort a terrific fire, driving the enemy out of the works three times and nearly destroying the fort, but each time they were reinforced by men from the destroyed *Merrimac* whose crew had been taken to Richmond.

"Towards the close of the battle when the ship was struck by four solid shot in less than a minute, exploding a shell between the decks, killing and wounding over twenty-eight men, a ten-pound cartridge exploded at the same instant. The ship was believed to be on fire.

"Corporal Jno. F. Mackie saw that the after 100-Pounder Parrott Rifle had lost its entire crew. Without orders, he took charge of the Rifle and called to his assistance a number of the Marine Guard. Succeeded in blowing up one of the enemy's casemates, destroying a 10-inch Columbiad that had been doing terrible execution on the ship every time it was fired. This gun had killed and wounded nearly every man in the after part of the ship, striking it in a vital place every time. The deck at this time was covered with dead and dying men, but he remained at his post until the close of the action doing excellent work with the Rifle.

"At noon the gunner, Mr. Boareum, reported that we had fired every round of ammunition in the magazine. At this moment we were struck by a number of solid shot that created terrible havoc on our deck. Captain Rodgers then gave orders to withdraw from the action. The vessel then retired in good order giving the enemy several parting shots that told severely upon the Fort.

"The *Monitor* withdrew early in the fight, not being able to give the required elevation to her guns. The *Naugatuck* burst her gun, a 100-Pounder Rifle, early in the action and left the fight. The *Port Royal* and the *Aroostook*, being wooden vessels, were also obliged to get out of the action early on account of the plunging fire, thus leaving the *Galena* all alone in the battle for the last three hours.

"Notwithstanding that the *Galena's* armor did not prove of scarcely any service to her, she fought the fort terrifically and tore it all to pieces. During the battle the *Galena* was struck one hundred and thirty times, killing and wounding over seventy of her crew of 130 men—blood flowed like water—and several times she was believed to be on fire. A number of daring acts were performed by the crew that seem incredible at this date. Every man was a hero, except one officer who was afterwards dismissed. Four of the enlisted men were promoted as officers and received the Naval Medal of Honor.

"During the month of May '62, we were attacked by the rebels six different times, who suffered severely for their temerity. June 26

" 'During the battle the Galena *was struck one hundred and thirty times, killing and wounding over seventy of her crew of 130 men. . . .' " So wrote the first marine awarded the Congressional Medal of Honor.—Guns of U.S.S.* Galena

(U.S. NAVY)

to July 1, the *Galena* participated in the Seven Days' Battle with the Army of the Potomac, during which time General George B. McClellan made his headquarters on board the U.S. Ship *Galena*. Corporal Mackie had charge of the property of the general during that entire time. During this series of engagements the *Galena* and the other vessels of the fleet were constantly engaged day and night. It is universally admitted by all who participated in those terrible battles that the energetic action of the Navy saved the Army of the Potomac.

"From the 1st of July until the close of that campaign the *Galena* was kept constantly engaged with the enemy, although the ship was almost a wreck. The guns had to be shored up to keep them in their places on deck.

"The *Galena* was ordered down to Fortress Monroe where she was visited by President Lincoln, the Secretary of the Navy Gideon Welles, together with a large company of distinguished gentlemen. They expressed the most unbounded praise of the valor and heroic conduct of the officers and men of the *Galena*'s crew. Four of the men were promoted as officers and presented with Medals of Honor. When Corporal Mackie was introduced to the President and to the Secretary of the Navy, he was personally complimented in very high terms, promoted to Orderly Sergeant, and ordered to be placed on the Roll of Honor in General Orders for his gallant conduct and services and signal acts of devotion to duty.

"Jno. F. Mackie was ordered to Norfolk Navy Yard and, on the 1st of May 1863, he was sent to New York with a detachment of Marines. On the 1st of June was ordered to take command of the Marine Guard of the U.S. Steamer *Seminole* which left New York a few days after and put into Philadelphia about the 25th of June, where she remained until after the Battle of Gettysburg doing guard duty on the Delaware River above the city, to the great relief of the citizens.

"The *Seminole* was then ordered to join Admiral Farragut on the Mississippi River where she arrived about the 1st of August. On the way to New Orleans she captured the Rebel Steamer *Charleston* after a sharp conflict, sending her a prize to New York where she arrived safely.

"About the 1st of September we were ordered to Sabine Pass, Texas, where we remained until the middle of February, 1864. During that time had a severe fight with the rebel fleet that undertook to raise the blockade. Several small vessels were captured by the rebels—but they were finally driven off with severe loss and we remained in full possession.

"At the beginning of April, 1864 the *Seminole* was ordered to Mobile Bay and remained there until after the Battle of Mobile Bay, the capture of the Rebel Ironclad Fleet, and the bombardment and capture of Fort Morgan and the entire series of rebel forts, four in number. After the works were in possession of the fleet the *Seminole* was set to work removing the torpedoes from the channel, a very dangerous work. For, during the performance of the work, one of them exploded, blowing a boat out of the water, killing and wounding every officer and man in the boat, seventeen in number.

"About the 1st of September the ship was ordered to the coast of Texas and rendered magnificent service in capturing blockade runners, destroying several, and sending a number to New Orleans as prizes—one, notably, the immense *Sir William Peel*, with 2,000 bales of cotton—a number of skirmishes of exciting character but of no great importance.

"On the 26th of May, 1865 the fleet had the honor to receive the surrender of General Kirby Smith and 20,000 men of the Rebel Army together with the full surrender of Galveston and the entire coast of Texas, with all of the forts and armament, when the 'Last Rebel Flag' was lowered and the last armed rebel soldier laid down his arms, and the *War was Over*.

"The *Seminole* was ordered north about the last of June, 1865 to the Port of Boston where we arrived on the 10th of September and were ordered out of commission and the crew honorably discharged from the U.S. Naval Service on the 24th of September, 1865.

"Orderly Sergeant John F. Mackie arrived home in New York City the next day after four years and five months active service during which time he participated in 16 general battles and over one hundred skirmishes without ever having received a scratch of any kind, was in the first fight of the war and present at the Last Surrender. Surely this is a magnificent record of service for his Country."

V I I

The Andrews Raid

"THE expedition itself, in the daring of its conception, had the wildness of a romance, while in the gigantic and overwhelming results which it sought, and was likely to accomplish, it was absolutely sublime."

Even today, over one hundred years after the event, one cannot quarrel too violently with these sentiments contained in the official report of the Judge Advocate General of the Army to the Secretary of War. The concept was truly daring, wildly romantic, and it has fired the imagination of people ever since.

There has been so much written about the Andrews Raid (which the Army Medal of Honor book calls the "Mitchell Raiding Party") it would seem there could be little new that could possibly be added to that story. Yet a book about the Medal of Honor in the Civil War can scarcely ignore the raid, for the first six men to be awarded the medal were soldiers who had taken part in that raid. They were presented their Congressional Medals of Honor on March 25, 1863, by Secretary of War Edwin M. Stanton in his office in Washington, then taken to the White House for a visit with President Abraham Lincoln. Their citation in the Army book is very simple:

"Nineteen of twenty-two men (including two civilians) who, by direction of General Mitchell (or Buell), penetrated nearly 200 miles south into the enemy's territory and captured a railroad train at Big Shanty, Ga., in an attempt to destroy the bridges and track between Chattanooga and Atlanta."

The trusting reader is inclined to take this statement at its face value. The next thing that he will probably do will be to peruse the list and even count the names. If he does, he will find that there are indeed nineteen names. As he studies the list he will discover that all of these soldiers were assigned to one of three Ohio infantry regiments. He may then determine which six were awarded their medals by Secretary Stanton on March 25, 1863, and learn that they were:

Private William Bensinger,	*Company G, 21st Ohio*
Private Robert Buffum,	*Company H, 21st Ohio*
Sergeant Elihu H. Mason,	*Company K, 21st Ohio*
Private Jacob Parrott,	*Company K, 33rd Ohio*
Sergeant William Pittinger,	*Company G, 2nd Ohio*
Corporal William H. Reddick,	*Company B, 33rd Ohio*

In the process, however, the reader will surely wonder why eight medals were awarded in September 1863, one on a specific date in that month (September 17), two during the month of July 1864, one on August 4, 1866, and the last one not until July 28, 1883, twenty-one years after the event. He may also wonder why the citation reads: "by direction of General Mitchell (or Buell)."

Perhaps, it will be remembered that eight of the party were hanged in Atlanta, Georgia. The natural assumption will be that those eight awarded the medal during the month of September 1863 were the eight who were executed. Obviously the War Department thoughtfully awarded them the next medals. The best way to check this fact is to refer to the book written by William Pittenger, the historian of the raid, one of the first six to receive the medal although the Army has his name incorrectly spelled. Of all the books written on the subject, Pittenger's book, published in 1887, entitled *Daring and Suffering*, is the most fascinating and accurate account.

From William Pittenger's book we soon learn that the War Department has managed to spell General Mitchel's name wrong, as well as Pittenger's, and we also learn that our natural assumption about the thoughtfulness of the War Department is 75 per cent in error. Only two of the eight medals awarded during the month of September 1863 went to the soldiers who had been hanged. By this time we are becoming a bit wary of making assumptions about War Department actions. Here again we are reminded of the curious wording of the War Department citations. The entire group of entries in the Army book is labeled "Mitchell Raiding Party" yet the citation reads "by direction of General Mitchell (or Buell)." Is the War Department unsure which general directed the raid?

The words "Nineteen of twenty-two men (including two civilians)" also claim our attention. Can it be that the War Department has failed to award the proper number of medals? Of course the Army could not have awarded the medal to the two civilians, but the numbers apparently indicate that there was one unfortunate soldier who never received his award. Were there some extenuating circumstances or, worse still, was one of the poor fellows who was hanged neglected? It would help to review the story of what happened.

While the great Battle of Shiloh was being fought on April 6–7, 1862, in western Tennessee, two men in eastern Tennessee were preparing a plan aimed at the capture of the city of Chattanooga. One of the men was Brigadier General Ormsby M. Mitchel who, at West Point, had been a classmate of General Robert E. Lee. Mitchel was a division commander in the Union army commanded by General Don Carlos Buell. The man with whom Mitchel was conferring was a Union secret agent named James J. Andrews. Together the two devised one of the most daring, unique exploits ever attempted in the history of warfare.

Briefly stated, the plan proposed by Mr. Andrews was that he and a small group of men should make their way secretly to a point over one hundred miles behind the Confederate lines, steal a train between Atlanta and Chattanooga, then dash madly back north, burning bridges and destroying telegraph wires as they went. It was hoped that, with Chattanooga thus temporarily isolated from the Confederacy, General Mitchel would be able to seize the city.

Twenty-four volunteers were initially assigned to take part in the expedition. Twenty-two of them slipped through the Confederate lines as far as Marietta, Georgia. Early in the morning of April 12, 1862, twenty boarded a northbound train as passengers, prepared to capture it when the opportunity arose. Two, unfortunately, missed the train; they arrived just as it was pulling out of the station. When the train crew stopped for breakfast, the twenty swiftly and silently uncoupled the passenger cars, climbed into the engine and into the freight cars, then raced northward toward Chattanooga.

The story of the race that followed constitutes one of the most thrilling passages in American history. The daring raiders almost succeeded in completing their fantastic plan. Unfortunately, for them, Andrews had postponed putting the plan into effect by one day. This delay was fatal.

General Mitchel had not been informed of the postponement. He advanced promptly on schedule toward Chattanooga on Friday, April 11. Thus on the following day, Saturday, April 12, there were extra trains on the road caused by the threat of General Mitchel's advance the day before. These extra trains slowed the raiders at intervals causing the loss of valuable time that could not be regained. This single factor might not have been enough to cause the failure of the expedition but at Big Shanty on Saturday the Andrews party had the misfortune of stealing the train of a conductor named William A. Fuller. Also on that train was Anthony Murphy, the foreman of the road machine shops. If Andrews had chosen the earlier day, Friday, his pursuers might not have been as determined and energetic. William A. Fuller was a worthy opponent and the presence of Murphy was invaluable in the great locomotive chase that followed. Though astounded to see his engine, the *General,* and part of his train disappearing in the distance, Fuller, Murphy, and the engineer started pursuit on foot, ignoring the laughter this spectacle aroused. They found a handcar, then an engine, finally a more powerful engine, the *Texas,* with which Fuller continued the pursuit, both parties at times reaching a speed of a mile a minute over a terribly war-worn track.

Under Andrews' direction the raiders did everything in their power to delay pursuit, removing rails, throwing obstacles onto the track, and attempting to burn the bridges but, here again, the loss of a day proved fatal. On Friday the weather had been clear with a strong wind; the old wooden bridges would have burned readily. But on Saturday the rain fell in torrents; the plan to burn the bridges utterly failed. Eventually Andrews and his men had to run for the woods; all twenty were captured plus the two who had been left behind at Marietta. Two months later, in June 1862, Andrews, another civilian, William Campbell, and six soldiers were executed. In October, after six months confinement, eight of the prisoners escaped. The last six were exchanged in March 1863, and became famous as the first soldiers in the United States Army to receive the Congressional Medal of Honor.

The names of these six men have already been given. Therefore the list below will include only the names of those who escaped from prison or who were hanged. Ignoring such discrepancies as middle initials, which have generally been resolved in favor of

The General *was not damaged in the raid but looked like this after becoming involved in an explosion of eighty-one carloads of ammunition on the night of September 1, 1864. Though torn and battered, the famed engine was soon back in service.*

Pittenger's book, and taking his spelling of "Robinson" rather than the Army's "Robertson," the men concerned were:

8 *Escaped from Prison, October, 1862*	*Medals Awarded*
Wilson W. Brown	September, 1863
Daniel A. Dorsey	September 17, 1863
Martin J. Hawkins	September, 1863
William Knight	September, 1863
John R. Porter	September, 1863
John A. Wilson	September, 1863
John Wollam	July 20, 1864
Mark Wood	September, 1863

This leaves the eight who were hanged. We may expect to find among their names the one soldier who was never awarded the medal.

Executed	*Medals Awarded*
James J. Andrews	Civilian (no medal)
William Campbell	Civilian (no medal)
Samuel Robinson	September, 1863
Marion A. Ross	September, 1863
John W. Scott	August 4, 1866
Perry G. Shadrack	_____
Samuel Slavens	July 28, 1883
George D. Wilson	_____

But this leaves *two* men who were hanged and never awarded the medal. If this be the case, who was the Army's 19th man? The name given is James Smith. He is listed as: "Private, Company I, 2nd Ohio Infantry," and the date of issue is given as "6 July 1864." We may search William Pittenger's book again and again, from cover to cover, and find no mention whatever of a James Smith, although Pittenger names every other person on the expedition and gives a great deal of information concerning each one involved. Since these total 22, James Smith cannot be one of them!

There is a possibility (and some writers on the subject have advanced the theory) that he was either the twenty-third or twenty-fourth volunteer originally assigned to the expedition, but who, for some unknown reason, never actually took part in the raid.

This is a pleasant and somewhat consoling thought when set against the disturbing fact that the War Department failed to take any action whatever in the case of either Perry G. Shadrack or George D. Wilson. Perhaps this idea was also in the minds of the officers

". . . the War Department failed to take any action whatever in the case of either Perry G. Shadrack or George D. Wilson."—No photograph has been located of Shadrack. This photograph of George D. Wilson, taken ten years before the war, is from William Pittenger's Daring and Suffering, *published in 1887.*
(LIBRARY OF CONGRESS)

who, in 1916 and 1917, reviewed the Medal of Honor records and left James Smith's name on the list.

Just what was the basis for the award? The answer can be found in the National Archives. James Smith's father wrote a letter applying for the medal, stating that his son had been in a Confederate prison, and had been one of the raiders. By this time, General Mitchel, the division commander, had died of yellow fever and his superior, General Buell, had been replaced by General Rosecrans. Under these conditions, the medal was awarded.

Perhaps James Smith was the twenty-third or twenty-fourth man in the famous raid but there is another interesting possibility. When the Judge Advocate General submitted his report to the Secretary of War, one person objected to it. That person was General Don Carlos Buell. His objection was twofold. First, he contended that the Andrews raid had not been organized by General Mitchel, but rather by Buell's chief of staff, Colonel James B. Fry. Secondly,

General Buell claimed that it was to have been a much smaller affair and that, if it had been conducted as planned, on a smaller scale, the chances for success would have been greater.

General Buell was confusing the larger Andrews raid with an earlier, less ambitious attempt conducted in March 1862 involving only eight men. William Pittenger also describes this effort in a supplement to his book, referring to this enterprise as the "First or Buell Railroad Raid." He identified six of these men but did not know the names of the other two. James Smith could have been the eighth man who took part in this expedition.

However, on James Smith's service record in the National Archives there is an entry indicating that he was on detached service from February 28 to May 31, 1862. This would seem to prohibit him from having taken part in either of the two Andrews raids, but there are still other possibilities. He could have participated in some other enterprise fostered by General Mitchel. Throughout the period of his command Mitchel proved again and again that he was the type of officer who believed in waging active warfare. The division that he commanded was constantly engaged in forward operations, harassing the enemy whenever practicable, and advancing into the enemy's territory at every opportunity. Any one of these operations could have caused Smith's father to refer to his son as one of the Mitchel raiders.

In addition, the official records mention a man by this name who was caught behind the lines under peculiar circumstances. He was put in a Confederate prison on suspicion of being a spy or a saboteur engaged in burning bridges. After a considerable lapse of time this James Smith was disposed of by sending him North.

Although there is no letter in the Kohen collection from James Smith, it is a pleasure to present the reply written by Wilson W. Brown, one of the train engineers, telling of his early life, touching briefly on the raid itself, then describing his escape and flight to the Union lines.

"Dowling, Wood County, Ohio
"December 27, 1889

"I was born in Fountain County, Indiana in the year 1839. When I was but eight years of age, my father moved to Logan County, Ohio. We had been in Ohio but one year when my father died. This was a dreadful misfortune as my father was a poor man and did not leave much of this world's goods to us.

"I at once saw the responsibility that fell upon me. My poor old mother, now bowed down with grief, and my little brothers and sisters who were younger than I, must be cared for. I at once sought work that I might aid them in their distress.

"I went to work in a brickyard at twenty-five cents per day, and this little sum was given to my mother as fast as I earned it. My ambition, however, led me away from the brickyard. I had a desire to learn something of mechanical engineering and, when twelve years of age, I went to learn all that was in my reach of stationary engineering. I seemed to be adapted to this pursuit and soon acquired a fair knowledge of the business.

"I was given a position as engineer at a sawmill at seventy-five cents per day which, to a lad of my age, seemed a princely sum. I remained two years at the sawmill, giving my undivided attention to the study of engineering. Every moment of time that I could devote to the study of books upon the subject was taken advantage of and, after two years' time in the sawmill, my aspirations led me to seek a position upon the railroad.

"A friend was an engineer on an Ohio road, and to him I went with a plea for an opportunity to handle the Iron Horse. I was promised the first vacancy that occurred in the position of fireman. The opportunity soon came and I was made fireman for my friend, the engineer. I was then sixteen years old. I worked in this position for one year. Then my friend aided me, by strong recommendations, to secure an engine. I put in a year or two as a full-fledged engineer. I then prepared for a trip to the South.

"After spending eight months as an engineer on a road running into New Albany, Indiana, I engaged as second engineer on a steamer from New Albany to New Orleans. From New Orleans I went to Mobile, Alabama, and I secured a position as engineer on the Mobile and Ohio Road. I remained on this road until late in 1860. When it looked as though war was going to be declared I left for my home in Ohio.

"It was some time before I reached home and, when I did, the drums were beating and the boys were marching away. In September, 1861, I enlisted as a private in Company F, 21st Ohio Volunteer Infantry for three years. The place where I enlisted was Findlay,

Hancock County, Ohio. Our regiment was assigned to that department known as the Cumberland, and I took part in the battles fought by that army.

"In 1862, when the famous Andrews Raid was organized, I went as engineer. The raiders were all captured and held as spies and,

" 'In 1862, when the famous Andrews Raid was organized, I went as engineer.' "
—Wilson W. Brown, from a wartime photograph that appeared in Pittenger's Daring and Suffering
(LIBRARY OF CONGRESS)

after eight of our number had been executed at Atlanta, Georgia, the remainder of us rushed upon the guards and disarmed them, and fled to the woods. Knight and I reached the Union lines after 48 days, travelling by night and secreting ourselves by day. Some nights we would travel hard all night and not get over eight or ten miles. We had to swim rivers, wade through swamps, and scale lofty mountains. In addition to this, we had to constantly be on the alert for the enemy, through whose lines we were slipping. Sometimes we felt as if our hearts would break. We were weak from fatigue and starvation, and were hounded by an enemy that clamored for our blood. We knew to be caught would be instant death, and our only watchword was: 'Forward—Forward.' No tongue can tell the suffering we endured on that dreary march, away in those dreary swamps in Georgia and Tennessee, through which we came. God only knows!

"We would sometimes stop and fix up as best we could at a place where, if possible, we could sleep for a little while to recuperate our exhausted energies. But sound sleep would not come. We would dream of bloodhounds in pursuit of us. We would dream of the huge scaffold that the rebels had erected near Atlanta, on which they executed eight of my comrades, and boasted that we should dangle on the same ropes. It is hard for one to sleep under such circumstances but, thank God, the hour of deliverance came.

"I reached the Union lines in safety and went directly to my regiment and took part in the Battle of Stones River. After this I went in person to General Rosecrans and asked him for a furlough home for 30 days. It was granted and I visited my home. While on this visit I was called to Washington to depose in regard to the raid. At Washington I was presented with a Medal of Honor by Mr. Stanton who was then Secretary of War. I also received a commission as a 2nd Lieutenant in F Company, 21st Ohio Volunteers. These honors were conferred upon me for distinguished services rendered on the Mitchel Raid. I returned from Washington to my home in Ohio and, before going to the front again, I was united in marriage to Miss Clarrisa Laman of Hancock County, Ohio. I remained at home only a short time after I was married before I went to the front again, leaving a loving wife, a mother, sisters, and brothers to mourn for me.

"I reached my regiment a few days previous to the Battle of Chickamauga. I went into battle with the boys and received two serious wounds, which rendered me unfit for further military duty. I returned to Columbus, Ohio, and was discharged, and went to my home in Hancock County, Ohio. I moved from there to Wood County, Ohio where I have resided ever since. My occupation has been, since discharge, farming. My wife and I have struggled on in life and have surmounted many difficulties, and have raised a large family of boys and girls, of whom we feel very proud.

"Very Respectfully
"*Wilson W. Brown*
"One of the Engineers of the Mitchel Raid."

VIII

Boys in Battle

VALOR came in surprisingly small packages during the great American conflict. Examination of the records reveals thousands of boys under eighteen who served in both the northern and southern armies, and several hundred of these were listed as only twelve to fifteen years old. In addition, there is no way of telling with any degree of accuracy how many other youngsters, eager to get into the war, lied to the recruiting officers about their age. Those who appeared to be approximately eighteen, or not too far from it, served in the ranks. Others, obviously younger, were usually carried on the rolls as musicians or drummer boys. In addition, numerous cases appear in newspaper stories of boys alleged to be from eight to twelve years old who were not enlisted but were permitted to tag along with the troops without any official status.

Undoubtedly the most famous of these boys was a youngster named Johnny Clem. Many people today think of him as "The Drummer Boy of Shiloh," identifying him as the hero of the song of the same name. It is true that Johnny was present at the battle but there is no particular reason to believe that the poet, Will S. Hays, had Johnny Clem in mind. There were many other drummer boys present at Shiloh. Johnny, age ten, could have been the youngest there. He had run away from home in May 1861 and, after an unsuccessful attempt to join the 3rd Ohio Volunteer Infantry as a drummer, was carried along by the 22nd Michigan as a sort of mascot. During the battle a shell smashed his drum, winning for him the nickname "Johnny Shiloh." Later, at the Battle of Chickamauga, Johnny grabbed a musket and shot a very surprised Confederate off his horse. After this exploit people began calling him "The Drummer Boy of Chickamauga." Although he was the best known of all the drummer boys, and was twice wounded in battle, Johnny was not awarded a Medal of Honor. After the war he received a commission and eventually retired as a major general.

Perhaps the most interesting case involving young boys was that of the Thompson brothers, because it is the only instance in history where two brothers won the medal. Allen and James Thompson of Sandy Creek, New York, were privates in Company K, 4th New York Heavy Artillery. They received the same citation for gallantry at the Battle of Five Forks, Virginia, April 1, 1865: "Made a hazardous reconnaissance through timber and slashings, preceding the Union line of battle, signaling the troops and leading them through the obstructions."

The youngest recipient of the Medal of Honor was Willie Johnston who was carried on the rolls as a musician in Company D of the 3rd Vermont Volunteers. Willie had been born in 1850 in Morristown, New York, but by the Civil War his family had moved to Vermont. At the beginning of the war, his father enlisted in the 3rd Vermont Infantry, then Willie joined the same unit to be near his father. Willie was decorated in 1863 for gallantry the year before in the Seven Days' Battle which marked the end of the Peninsular Campaign of 1862. At that time he could not have been over twelve years old.

By a strange coincidence, the 3rd Vermont Infantry carried on its rolls another youngster who won the medal for bravery in the same campaign. For his part in the action at Lees Mills on April 16, 1862, Julian A. Scott, who had enlisted at fifteen, and was then only sixteen, was cited for gallantry by the War Department: "Crossed the creek under a terrific fire of musketry several times to assist in bringing off the wounded."

Julian Scott was one of the more modest heroes:

"The service for which the medal was given me was not extraordinary—simply for doing my duty as a musician in looking after the wounded at the fight of Lees Mills, April 16, 1862. I deserved the reward no more than any of my comrades who were engaged in that affair; but it happened that I was the only musician there for duty. I think any of the others would have done the same had they been on hand. The order for attack was unexpected and but four companies of our regiment crossed over, numbering 192 officers and men. The loss in killed and wounded was 45 per cent. . . . The initial *A* was an addition at enlistment. My baptismal name is simply Julian Scott."

On the form furnished him, Scott also wrote: "At Lees Mills my haversack was nearly rendered useless by one of the enemy's bullets. Was slightly wounded at White Oak Swamp and at Drewry's Bluff but hardly worth mentioning."

At the end of April 1863 Julian Scott, age seventeen, was discharged. He went to New York City to begin the study of art under Emmanuel Leutze who is most famous for his painting of Washington Crossing the Delaware. After working with Leutze for a year, Scott returned to the army as a civilian, and became a volunteer aide on the staff of General William F. "Baldy" Smith, where he devoted most of his time to making sketches of soldier life.

Only three days after the engagement at Lees Mills, a drummer boy in Company B of the 9th New York Volunteers, popularly known as Hawkins' Zouaves, earned a Medal of Honor, and again the War Department made a mistake in its bookkeeping. This time the error was not in the recording of the name and initials but in the computation of his age.

J. C. Julius Langbein did not write a letter describing the winning of his award but instead sent some newspaper clippings and filled out the form that had been mailed to him. Born in Germany on September 29, 1845, J. C. Julius Langbein had enlisted at age fifteen, and promptly became known to the men of his company as "Jennie" because of his small stature and slender, girlish appearance. But, by April 19, 1862, when he performed the act for which he was later decorated, he was actually sixteen years old. The citation, however, says that at Camden, North Carolina, "A drummer boy, 15 years of age, he voluntarily and under a heavy fire went to the aid of a wounded officer, procured medical assistance for him, and aided in carrying him to a place of safety." The intriguing part of the story is that the officer whose life Julius saved was the very one who, just before the regiment left for the war, had promised Julius' mother that he would look after and take care of her boy.

Myron H. Ranney, of Franklinville, New York, also fought in the Peninsular Campaign where he was wounded in the leg but recovered sufficiently to take part in the Second Battle of Bull Run.

"I entered the Bull Run battle August 30, '62 with my company on the right of the colors and, being young, only 17, my place was on the left of my company.

"The color sergeant and the entire color guard of eight men

" '. . . I was the only musician there for duty. I think any of the others would have done the same had they been on hand.' "—Julian A. Scott
(KOHEN COLLECTION)

" '. . . he voluntarily and under a heavy fire went to the aid of a wounded officer . . .' "—Newspaper sketch of Julius Langbein
(KOHEN COLLECTION)

were killed or wounded as fast as they took the colors. In fact, more than ¾ths of the entire company to which I belonged were disabled or killed, and the whole regiment fared the same.

"Our flag was so torn to pieces that it could hardly be recognized, and was lying within a few feet of the rebel line of battle, and not a Bluecoat within thirty feet of it. When I first noticed the Old Flag was in danger of going into the hands of the enemy, I went alone to its rescue. Received a wound in my right arm, and how I ever lived one minute in such a hail of bullets, I cannot tell.

"Captain Savage started to come to my aid and was nearly cut in two with bullets. Captain Carl Hess of Company G started to come to me, was wounded, and then sang out to me to lie down. I had been on my feet up to this time. Another officer (Lieutenant Burnell I think) was also hurt trying to help me. Then at the last moment, although very tardily, when it seemed to me I was gone, and the whole command, or what was left of it, should have come to the rescue of the standard, one George Stoddard came to help me. He relieved me of the flag; and he and I went off the field together.

"I was paraded to the brigade and regiment. Captain Hess and Colonel Marshall wanted to promote me to color sergeant, but it was finally decided that I was too young, not tall enough, and I don't know what all. George Stoddard was made color sergeant while I remained in the ranks to the end of the war and was finally mustered out as such. But of one thing I am proud, and that is I always did my duty as a private. I am happy to say that the war records will bear me out. I am one of a few privates to receive the Medal of Honor. And if the Pension Department will do me justice and help in my declining years I will not regret what I did toward putting down the Rebellion. The Old Flag I saved at Bull Run can still be seen in the Court House at Rochester, New York.

"The inscription on my medal reads: 'The Congress to Private Myron H. Ranney, Co. G, 13th N.Y. Vols. for Gallantry at Bull Run, Va., Aug. 30th, 1862.'"

"It is only proper to bring all such facts relating to our late war before this generation of boys."

Undoubtedly Robinson B. Murphy, writing from Columbus, Ohio, on October 1, 1890, was thinking of the valor displayed by the boys of his generation but then, instead of furnishing a sketch of the service for which his medal was awarded, he told of the problems he encountered in persuading his family to let him enlist.

" 'Our flag was so torn to pieces that it could hardly be recognized . . .' "
—*Collo-type illustrating the Second Battle of Bull Run, made by Wells and Hope*

"In Oswego, Illinois, a little town about forty-five miles from Chicago, Robinson B. Murphy was born. His father was one of the most respected men in the county, a lawyer by profession, and, we believe, the first sheriff elected on the Republican ticket in that county. In 1861, when the first call was made for soldiers, Bob declared his intentions to go to war, being then only twelve years old. His parents and friends laughed at him. Soon after that Bob was missing. He had walked across country about eighteen miles to join the 20th Illinois. His father, learning his whereabouts, sent a man after him with instructions to bring him home and of course Bob had to return. In the spring of '62 another opportunity presented itself in the shape of a recruiting officer who agreed to take

him as a drummer boy. He started again, but, while he was at the depot waiting for a train, some of his young friends had informed his father and once more he was marched back home.

"Bob's father being a politician and a strong-minded man was making many war speeches and had helped to raise several companies for the war. One evening in August '62 a great war meeting was held at the Court House in Oswego. . . . Bob's father . . . was immediately called upon for a speech. He responded by saying: 'I have urged many to go to the war in defense of our country. Now I propose to head this list and go myself.' Bob, being by his father's side, was of course ready and anxious to do the same thing. . . . There seemed to be no use trying to explain or reason with him, for he was bound to go. On the 6th day of August with his father's consent he was enlisted as a drummer boy at the age of thirteen years, two months, and twenty-four days."

On July 28, 1864, almost exactly two years later, Robinson Murphy, musician, Company A, 127th Illinois Infantry, found himself serving as aide to his brigade commander. Following the Battle of Atlanta, fought on July 22nd, the Union armies had been engaged in drawing their lines closer around the city and in making a turning movement to the west to strike at the railroad supplying the southern forces. Suddenly, on July 28, a strong Confederate attack had been hurled against this turning movement. Union reinforcements were urgently needed at the front. Young Murphy, who knew the way, hastily volunteered. He led two regiments to their places in time for them to help turn the tide of battle. As if to prove that this assignment was not without its dangers, the War Department record noted that when the regiment reached the line of battle their guide, Robinson Murphy, promptly lost his horse—shot from under him. The boy, fifteen years old, lived to tell the tale and be decorated for valor twenty-six years later.

George Dallas Sidman was awarded the Medal of Honor for distinguished bravery at the Battle of Gaines' Mill, Virginia, June 27, 1862.

"The subject of this sketch was born at Rochester, New York, November 25, 1844 and was therefore but a youth when, on April 19, 1861, he answered the President's first call for troops by enlisting at Owosso, Michigan as a drummer in a local company known as the 'Owosso Grays.'

"This company was never called into service but kept up its organization and regular drills until disbanded in July following. Young Sidman then went to Flint, Michigan, and on August 1, 1861 enlisted as a drummer of Company C, Stockton's Independent Michigan Volunteers, afterward designated the 16th Michigan Volunteer Infantry. After his regiment reached the front in the fall of 1861 it was discovered that Company C had more than its quota of musicians, and inasmuch as Sidman had not developed much merit as a drummer he was ordered to be discharged and sent home.

"This order nearly broke his heart and he begged piteously to be retained in service, offering to take a gun and perform a soldier's duty, if permitted to do so. This request, after some circumlocution, was granted, but his name was continued on the rolls as a drummer for some months longer in order to let him *grow* to a soldier's stature.

"The youngest and smallest *man* in the regiment, his position was on the extreme left of his company, which being the 'Color' company brought him shoulder to shoulder with the Color Guard, causing his diminutiveness to be most pronounced, side by side with the picked men of the regiment.

"The battle of Gaines' Mill, Virginia, the second of the Seven Days' Battles before Richmond, fought June 27, 1862, was where Comrade Sidman won the Medal he now so proudly wears, although subsequent acts entitled him to equal recognition. This battle was fought entirely by Fitz-John Porter's Division of 18,000 men, pitted against 'Stonewall' Jackson's Corps numbering 60,000 of the boasted 'foot cavalry.'

"Dan Butterfield's Light Brigade, composed of the 12th, 17th and 44th New York Infantry, the 83rd Pennsylvania Infantry, and the 16th Michigan Infantry, occupied the extreme left flank, forming a horseshoe curve, and resting on the border of Chickahominy Swamp. The sun was yet high in the heaven on that eventful day when Jackson hurled four solid columns against a weakened point in the centre of the line, and, enfilading it in both directions, soon

" 'The sun was yet high in the heaven on that eventful day when Jackson hurled four solid columns against a weakened point in the centre of the line . . .' "—Pencil and Chinese white drawing by Alfred R. Waud of the Battle of Gaines' Mill, June 27, 1862

(LIBRARY OF CONGRESS)

scattered our forces into the swamp. The stampeders, turned from a direct retreat to the rear by the enfilading movement of the enemy, crushed into the lines of Butterfield's brigade and nearly carried it into the swamp.

"Here, however, under the guidance of Butterfield[*] and a few daring officers, a remnant of the brigade was rallied, and with loud cheers charged back to their old positions, meeting and driving the enemy back at the points of their bayonets.

"It seemed like a 'forlorn hope' for this handful of brave men to meet a victorious foe on such terms, but gaining an advantageous position, they held it until darkness set in. History has never recorded this charge because there were none but the participants therein to tell the story, nevertheless time can never efface from the memory of the few survivors of that charge the then feeling that nothing but death could result to all.

"In the struggle with the stampeders in the swamp, young Sidman clung to a sapling until the crowd had passed, and then in answer to the rallying cries of the officers, he hurried to the 'Colors' of his regiment, and when the order was given to charge, was one of the first to respond calling upon his comrades to *'come ahead.'* He was severely wounded by a minnie ball through the hip in the almost hand to hand engagement that followed, but held to his gun and remained in the ranks until he fell fainting from over-exertion and weakness of his wounded limb. Dragging himself to an open ditch in the rear, he clubbed his musket over a stump to destroy its usefulness to the enemy, and throwing his accoutrements in the ditch, he crawled on his hands and knees off the field of battle and through Chickahominy Swamp. Was picked up the next day and carried to Savage's Station where two days later he was taken prisoner with 3,000 sick and wounded comrades left by McClellan to the tender mercies of the enemy. Here on June 29th he lay with other comrades under a large tree in the yard of the Savage House, exposed and between the two fires of the battle that was, on that day, fought over their heads.

"On July 4th he was conveyed to Richmond, and placed in Libby prison from which place a few days later he was sent to

* General Butterfield was also awarded the Medal of Honor for bravery in this battle. His citation read: "Seized the colors of the 83rd Pennsylvania Volunteers at a critical moment and, under a galling fire of the enemy, encouraged the depleted ranks to renewed exertion."

Castle Thunder, and thence to Belle Isle, from which pen, on August 18th, he was taken to City Point and exchanged.

"Being yet greatly disabled and hardly able to stand up on account of his wound, he was taken to Hammond General Hospital at Point Lookout, Maryland for treatment. The solitude of this place, with the war of the ocean and sighing of the wind through the pine trees surrounding the hospital, so affected his nervous system that he was nearly driven insane and begged to be transferred to some other place. This request being refused, he slipped by the guards one night and took passage in the stoke-hole of a Potomac River Steamboat going to Washington, where he arrived next day.

"The city was full of sick and wounded soldiers who had been sent back from the battle of Second Bull Run, fought a day or two before, and he had no difficulty in getting passed along the streets, hobbling on crutches.

"He reported to the general commanding the department, and requested to be sent to a hospital, frankly stating that he had eloped from Hammond Hospital, and his reasons for so doing. The general laughed heartily at his appearance which was anything but prepossessing after his night's escapade and torture in a bin of soft coal. As the hospitals of Washington were crowded with the sick and wounded and thousands were lying out of doors in the parks waiting for transportation elsewhere, there was no place for him to be sent except to the Convalescent Camp at Alexandria, to which place he was taken under guard.

"A few days later the Army of the Potomac arrived in front of Washington and proceeded to follow Lee into Maryland. Hearing that his regiment was encamped at Hall's Hill, a few miles distant, our young hero again eloped and after much effort found his way to the command. His return to the regiment with an open and discharging wound, as he then had, was a feat that few men would care to undertake, but when he announced that he had returned for *duty* the officers of his company refused to accept his services and the surgeon declared that he must not be permitted to remain. He obstinately refused however to go to the hospital again, and as the command was under marching orders, and did start on the Antietam Campaign next day, it was thought best to humor him for the time being, everybody believing that he must necessarily stay in the rear from lack of physical ability to march and keep up.

" '. . . there was no place for him to be sent except to the Convalescent

"Nothing daunted, however, when he saw his comrades marching away, and unable to keep up, he hailed a passing surgeon and asked to be put in an ambulance to cross the river. The surgeon, after examining his wound and listening to a cock-and-bull story of

*Camp at Alexandria, to which place he was taken under guard.'"—Known
to the soldiers as "Camp Misery"*

how he had been left by the surgeon of his regiment to shift for
himself, had him placed in an ambulance with orders to 'drop him
out' at Georgetown, 'after crossing Acqueduct Bridge.' He remained
in the ambulance all day, however, and much to the surprise of

officers and comrades appeared at the bivouac that evening in time to claim and receive his three days' rations then being issued. The next morning while the army was preparing to move he found a condemned horse by the wayside, and without much difficulty 'surrounded and captured him.'

"Piling a lot of discarded blankets upon the humps of his prize, to relieve the monotony of the situation so to speak, and using a number of knapsack straps, buckled and tied together for a bridle, he managed to get up quite a rig. There was no danger of the horse running away! In fact the principal danger was that he might *blow* away, as he had the heaves very bad and was exceedingly emaciated especially along the spine. The appearance of this *platoon* of 'Light Horse' in bivouac that night created much merriment among the comrades, and no little concern to the field officers, who had horses of their own, and not until it was fully decided that the animal was free from a contagious disease was he permitted to picket in the bivouac and sleep in peace. Sidman had developed a means to *remain* with his command and his officers and comrades were loud in their approval of his patriotism and faithfulness to duty. He was permitted to ride his horse when and where he pleased, often much to his own physical discomfort however, but always to the amusement of his comrades, who managed to 'forage' enough feed to make 'Old Crow' glad when he got into bivouac at night. No horse in all that army had better care and more feed on that march to Antietam. 'Old Crow' carried his gallant captor to Antietam Creek and on the morning of that memorable 17th of September 1862, while the army was drawn up in line of battle he was turned loose and never again seen by his grateful rider.

"On the morning of December 13, 1862, while the old Fifth Corps was drawn up in line of battle on Stafford Heights, waiting to cross the Rappahannock and enter Fredericksburg, Colonel Stockton commanding the Third Brigade, First Division called upon the 16th Michigan for a volunteer to carry the new brigade flag that had just reached the command.

"Sidman, now partly recovered from his wound, immediately sprang from the ranks and begged the privilege of this duty. His patriotism and fidelity to duty, well known to Colonel Stockton, won for him the coveted prize, much to the chagrin of several other comrades who valiantly offered their services.

"Leading the brigade in the last charge on Marye's Heights that memorable day he was again wounded, but not so severely as to prevent him from planting his 'colors' within one hundred and fifty yards of the enemy's lines where they remained thirty hours.

"Three days later he proudly bore his flag, with shattered shaft and pierced with several bullets, back across the Rappahannock, being one of the last to cross the river, his brigade having been detailed to cover the retreat.

"It was in this battle on Sunday, December 14th, while the brigade lay hugging the ground behind the slight elevation of earth a few yards in front of the enemy, and momentarily expecting an attack, that young Sidman, with another daredevil comrade of his regiment, displayed his humanity as well as his heroic valor, by running the gauntlet through the railway cutting for canteens of water for his sick and wounded comrades, this too at a time when a change from a prostrate to an upright position meant almost certain death at the hands of the enemy's sharpshooters, who were so stationed as to command the railroad cutting and the ground at the rear of the Union lines. Thirty years afterward, at the great Encampment of the G.A.R. at Washington, D.C. (September 19–25, 1892) where the survivors of this brigade held a reunion, Comrade Sidman presented to the Association a duplicate of the flag with which he had led the brigade up Marye's Heights on that memorable occasion.

"Soon after the battle of Fredericksburg our young hero was promoted to Corporal and returned to his company and was then regularly detailed as one of the Regimental Color Guard. He was with his command at Chancellorsville, Kelly's Ford, and Middleburg, Virginia. At the last named battle, fought June 21, 1863, while in the front rank of the Color Guard, charging and driving the enemy's cavalry from behind stone walls, he was wounded by a carbine ball through his right foot. After several months' treatment and sick furlough, he returned to his regiment the following December, but his wounds so afflicted him that he was unable to perform any duty.

"His old hip wound having broken open, began discharging pieces of bone and he was condemned for field service. He was offered his discharge, but declined it hoping the advent of warm weather might find him able to return to duty. In February, 1864, much to his disgust and against his protest, he was transferred to the Invalid Corps, where he remained until November 14, 1865, when honorably mustered out of service, having served almost continuously from April 19, 1861.

"While in the Invalid Corps and stationed in Washington, D.C. in 1865, he was a witness and an orderly for the court that tried and condemned the conspirators for the assassination of President Lincoln, and was present when Mrs. Surratt and her co-conspirators were hung. He was also a witness to the hanging of Wirz, the notorious Andersonville prison keeper.

"Since the war Comrade Sidman has held several important Government positions. In 1866 he was appointed Ass't. Assessor of Internal Revenue at Bay City, Michigan. In 1867 he was nominated and confirmed U.S. Consul to Mecklinburgh, Schwerin, Germany, which office was soon afterward abrogated because of the confederation of the German dependencies. In 1877 he went to South Africa on a gold and diamond prospecting expedition, and was in that country three years.

"He was there during the Zulu War and distinguished himself by offering to penetrate King Cetawayo's kraals and bring back information greatly desired by the British authorities, but being regarded as a 'Yankee adventurer,' his offer was declined.

"He, with four other Americans, organized an expedition across the Limpopo and spent several months in the 'Lo Bingulo' country, of Mashmaland and the Makapans between the Limpopo and Zambesi rivers.

"Returning to this country in 1880 he sought a Gov't appointment in one of the departments in Washington, and was rewarded with a clerkship in the Pension Bureau. Since 1882 to the present time (1894) he has been a Special Examiner of Pensions."

I X

The Vicksburg Storming Party

"ON THE morning of May 22, 1863, Lieutenant George H. Stockman of our company asked me if I did not wish to volunteer to go to a storming party. . . ."

Of all the descriptions written thirty years after the event, this letter by Joseph S. Labille of Vandalia, Illinois, best captures the spirit in which this enterprise was conceived. Too many of the others involved wrote of it as a "forlorn hope," but their descriptions were obviously deeply colored by memories of the disaster which occurred. Ex-private Labille did a much more effective job of re-creating the mood and feelings of those involved in the attack planned for that day.

When General Ulysses S. Grant ordered a second assault on the defenses of Vicksburg, to be launched on May 22, 1863, he knew that he had under his command an army supremely confident of victory. After months of frustrating efforts to get close to the enemy citadel, they were now ready to complete the task. The long-awaited goal was at last in sight. Under General Grant's direction, in a lightning-swift campaign they had defeated their enemy at every turn. In just eighteen days this army had won five battles and imprisoned the enemy behind the fortifications of Vicksburg. To complete their triumph they had only to assault the Confederate defensive lines now confronting them. The first attack of May 19, 1863, had failed, but this was no reason to feel discouraged, for the full power of all three Union corps had not been employed. The men were flushed with victory and felt certain that, if a fully co-ordinated assault were launched, it would surely succeed.

Thus, in a somewhat lighthearted manner, the troops of Grant's army approached the task set before them. They reckoned without the oft-demonstrated courage of the southern soldier who, though defeated in each of the preceding battles, was still ready to fight

"In just eighteen days this army had won five battles and imprisoned the enemy behind the fortifications of Vicksburg."—Wood engraving of the Siege of Vicksburg, from a sketch by Theodore R. Davis, Harper's Weekly

again. Some of the more experienced northern generals were not quite so certain of the results that could be expected from an attack against such formidable defenses. Furthermore, they were more inclined to remember how often in the past these same opponents had thwarted their efforts at every turn. With these thoughts in mind, General Frank P. Blair's division of Sherman's 15th Army Corps, which had an unusually strong point to attack, made some rather special preparations. In later years some confusion appears to have arisen as to the units involved in this volunteer storming party. All who participated were from General Blair's division but other soldiers from the 13th Army Corps, farther to the south, who were not members of this storming party, were also awarded Medals of Honor for this action.

The plan and the results may best be described by the participants. Individual versions differ as to the number of men involved and the number of casualties sustained by the storming party. With several accounts to choose from, it is difficult to decide which to present first, but, having begun with Joseph Labille of the 6th Missouri Infantry, it seems most appropriate to continue with his version.

"On the morning of May 22, 1863, Lieutenant George H. Stockman of our company asked me if I did not wish to volunteer to go to a storming party to keep a certain fort from firing its cannons while our army made a charge on the enemy's works. He told me that he had volunteered to go and wanted one man from our company to go with him. I then told him that I would go with him, and that I would go where he did. So, early in the forenoon, we reported for that purpose and soon after made the charge.

"The lieutenant, a brave fellow, fell wounded on the way. I went within 10 or 15 yards of the fort when a ball passed so close to my eyes that it completely blinded me. I ran against a bank of earth where a wounded soldier was sitting. He grasped me by the coat and told me to sit by him, that there was not much danger there. I bathed my eyes and in a few minutes I recovered my eyesight. Thus the boys got on top of the fort before I did. Then I made a dash for the top of the fort and got there.

"We lay flat on the top, keeping our muskets always ready. We lay there in the hot burning sun within 3 or 4 feet of the enemy, keeping them from firing their cannons. After we had been there some time the commanding officer in the fort said to us: 'Say, boys, I mean you Yankee boys, you must be a brave lot of men to have come where you are. You are all entirely at our mercy, but if you want to surrender to us, we will treat you with the very best we have in Vicksburg. You can come in at the right angle of the fort; there is a cannon hole to let you in.' I am not positive, but I think it was a man belonging to our regiment who cried out: 'Poke your head up here and we will show you whether we came here to surrender to you or not.' The Rebel officer then threatened to make a charge on us; some of our men told him to charge and be done.

"Sometime in the afternoon our army made the charge but did

not succeed in reaching us, though we kept that fort silent. . . . We remained there until dark when a lieutenant of some other regiment came and told us to make our way back the best we could. I do not know how the other boys got back but I got across the ditch and jumped a fence. While I jumped the fence I was fired at and had a very narrow escape. I got lost but finally found my company between twelve and one o'clock that night. I was reported killed but the boys were happy to see me alive again. I never found out how many got killed and wounded, but most of them were mowed down before we got to the fort. Some years ago I could have given you a much better report but I have forgotten a great deal since that occurrence. That is where I earned my Medal of Honor which I am very proud of. I send you my photo by mail, be sure and return it.

"Your Truly,
"Joseph S. Labille

"P.S. On the Army Muster Roll they have me born in France. As I spoke the French language, the officers, of course, thought I was a Frenchman. When I found it out, they told me it was too late to change it, as one of the rolls had gone to the State of Missouri, and one to Washington. So it remains as they had it down." (Labille had been born in Belgium in 1837.)

Labille also furnished, for the record, a copy of the furlough which he received. This consideration had been promised to all who would take part in this attack. In addition, he might have mentioned, but did not, that the War Department had also spelled his name wrong, as La Bill, and so it remains on all the record books.

The confusion created by the award of the Medal of Honor to certain individuals of the 13th Army Corps is further compounded by the citation of Captain Richard H. Wood who "led the 'volunteer storming party.'" He undoubtedly was a brave officer, but he was not the leader of this particular assault. The following letter from Private Wilson McGonagle of the 30th Ohio, and the reports in the official records, credit a different individual with being the leader, an officer who incidentally never received the coveted award.

"At Vicksburg, Mississippi, at 10 o'clock, May 22, 1863, an assault was ordered along the entire line. In front of General Frank P. Blair's division the assault was made in column on a large fort.

"Two (2) volunteers from each company in the division were called for to the number of 150 to carry boards and ladders to bridge the ditch and scale the fort. Captain Groce of the 30th Ohio Infantry led the storming party. Perhaps one-half of the 150 were killed or wounded before we reached the fort. The awful storm which greeted us made the assault a failure. The survivors each received a furlough and a few weeks ago we received a medal from Congress. Enclosed you will find my photograph. I believe I have covered the whole ground of your inquiry."

It should be noted here that Wilson McGonagle's statement that 150 men took part in the attack agrees with the reports submitted by his commanders. However, most of the others who participated give higher figures of the numbers involved.

Another brief account was submitted by James S. Cunningham, a farmer born in Washington County, Pennsylvania, who had enlisted at Bloomington, Illinois. This man apparently liked to move around the country. At the time of the battle he was serving in Company D, 8th Missouri Infantry, but after the war settled in Burlington, Kansas. His estimate of the number of men involved in the storming party is much closer to the figures given by the other members of the storming party, but his idea of the number of casualties sustained appears extraordinarily high.

"On May 22, 1863, when Grant made his second attack on Vicksburg, Colonel Coleman called for volunteers to go ahead of the main column with scaling ladders and guns, and storm the works in front of Vicksburg. I was one of 226 that volunteered out of the 15th Army Corps for that purpose. We were ordered to enter Vicksburg and plant our flag upon the court house, which, however, we failed to do. As the fire was so intense, we were obliged to retreat. There were only 20 of us got back alive, after which we laid siege on Vicksburg which lasted for 46 days."

One of those who "got back alive" had this to say about his experience.

"I had 21 bullets through my clothes, three through my hat, and nary a one touched the hide. But I got it the next day in the trenches. I was struck in the shoulder. It was a flesh wound. Then, on the 24th, I got it in the leg; then, on the 25th, I got it in the hip. That is all the wounds I got."

James M. McClelland of the 30th Ohio must have been a rugged, determined individual. Despite his wounds received at Vicksburg, he went on "with Sherman to the sea."

A dramatic account was furnished by former private Andrew E. Goldsbery of Company E, 127th Regiment Illinois Volunteers.

"The morning of May 22, 1863, General Grant's army, in the rear of Vicksburg, was getting into line for another grand charge. Our regiment had got into position about 9 a.m. Soon after we were in line, the adjutant passed down and stopped at the head of each company.

"After passing by our company the captain read the following order: 'One volunteer from each company in the division is called for, to make a charge with fixed bayonets. Volunteers will carry scaling ladders to be placed on the works. You will be supported by a brigade. The survivors will receive promotions and will be given 30 days furlough.'

" 'Now, boys, who will volunteer?' I waited until the second call and replied, 'Goldsbery is ready to go.'

"At 10 a.m. the order was given to charge. It seemed that the sun never shone so beautiful as it did that morning. Life never seemed so sweet; the least fear never came over me. I felt as cool as if on dress parade; but yet, as I looked down the line of less than 200 as brave men as ever stood on American soil, I realized that many of us had but an hour to live. We well knew what was before us. We had fought over the same battlefield before, but three days preceding. Many of our comrades' blood had stained these hills.

"But the order comes: 'Right-face, Forward, Double-quick March!' My position was very near the front of the column. As we came over the first ridge, there was scarcely an enemy to be seen. We crossed through intervening hills that were filled with fallen timber, and came to the last raise before the works. It might have been 200 feet. I had made the calculations that they would fire over the front of the column. As we reached the raise of the hill the works were covered with men. Every one was looking down the sight of his gun, with finger on the trigger. The black muzzles of the cannon were loaded with grape and canister. Not a muscle moved 'til the command: 'Ready, Fire.'

"And then it seemed like a sheet of fire, a tremendous roar. For an instant I was senseless. I thought I was going over and over. I fell close to the edge of the trench. When I recovered my scattered senses, I could see our flag ahead. I gave a jump into the trench. Our color bearer planted the flag on top of the enemy's works, where it remained all day. It was useless for us to attempt to do any more with scarce a dozen of our number left. We crouched under the bank. We could do no more. Our support was driven back.

"It was pitiful to hear the cries of the wounded and then there was a moment's lull. A shell with short fuse came rolling down on us. But one of our number who had served in the artillery cried:

" 'A shell with short fuse came rolling down on us.' "—Wood engraving made from a drawing by F. B. Schell, in Portfolio of War and Nation, *edited by General Marcus J. Wright*

(FORT WARD MUSEUM)

'Throw it back. They can't cut their fuse short enough to hurt us.'
After a few were thrown back they stopped that.

"When the brigade fell back and it became quiet we talked back
and forth with the Johnnies. They told us we would be taken in
after dark. When it came to the afternoon charge, which was by
Grant's whole army simultaneously at 2 p.m., we heard a great com-
motion among the Johnnies and our own big guns began to fire
rapidly. We were in more danger as the shells struck in the bank
over our heads, and some fell short. We dug under the bank as a
means of protection from them. Two of us were sharing a hole in
partnership. We held a council of war and resolved that on the first
fire of the Rebs, under cover of the smoke, we would make a break
for the rear which we did, and reached a log about 100 feet from
the fort. We fired as rapidly as we could load during the afternoon
charge 'til a shell struck so close to us from our own guns we had
to fall back, after getting out of the trench in front of the enemy's
works, which I think was about 12 feet wide and 4 or 5 feet deep.
The fort might have been 15 feet above the raise of the trench.
After we fell back we could see the terrible results of the charge. I
never saw men lay so thick. The whole column was swept down 'til
the hill was crimson with their blood, 'til I could not bear the sight,
and was thankful I had escaped. But it might be only for a moment. . . .

"Of all my experience on the field of battle, I had never seen
the horrors of a great charge before. We read in history of the great
cavalry charge of Balaclava in the Crimea . . . but they did no
greater deed than that little band on the 22nd of May, 1863."

In the reports of this assault two names stand out above all the
rest: Captain Groce and Private Trogden. The division commander,
Major General Frank P. Blair, began his description of the action
with these words: "At the signal the volunteer storming party, led
by Captain John H. Groce, of General Ewing's brigade, dashed forward in gallant style, and planted the flag of the Union, which was
borne by Private Howell G. Trogden, of the Eighth Missouri, upon
the bastion of the enemy."

Captain Groce was wounded when he reached the parapet but
managed to make his way back to his own lines that evening. This
gallant officer continued to fight his country's battles until, on De-

cember 13, 1864, he was killed in the attack that captured Fort
McAllister, Georgia. It is a real tragedy that, over thirty years later,
when Congressional Medals of Honor were awarded to the Vicksburg storming party, people still thought of medals as awards for
the living. Thus the name of John H. Groce, who led the attack,
will never appear on the list of those who have received the country's highest award for valor.

Fortunately, Private Trogden, a southern boy from Randolph
County, North Carolina, survived to apply for his medal, so that
his description, a vivid personal account, has been preserved. Included with his letter was a patriotic poem written by O. B. Hale
of Lexington, Kentucky, which had been published in the New York
Herald shortly after the battle.

"On the 22nd of May, '63, a detail was called for out of our regiment but, for what, we did not know. There were 22 volunteers
from our regiment. We were ordered to take a hundred rounds of
ammunition, 40 in our cartridge box and 60 in our pockets. We were
then marched up in front of General Grant's headquarters where
we stacked arms. We here met details from other regiments which
swelled the number to 250 all told. Generals Grant, Sherman, Logan, Ewing, Steele, F. P. Blair and others were there. 'Attention'
was called and General Sherman made a short speech. Pointing to
the fort, he told us we were there as a forlorn hope, that we were
to file to the right, and go into the mouth of the cut where we
would be provided with scaling ladders.

"I noticed that there was no one bearing the flag. Then I cried
out to General Sherman: 'Say, General, won't it be advisable for
someone to carry a flag? If we get scattered we will see something
to rally to.' About 20 yards from us there was a fine silk flag set in
the ground in front of some general's headquarters. General Sherman walked over and, taking the flag, brought it to me saying in a
jovial manner: 'It's a dangerous job, my boy, to try to put that flag
on that fort.' We then marched into the cut and waited the signal
for the charge on the fort, with our improvised scaling ladders.

"At 10 o'clock we heard the boom of the cannon which was our
signal to charge. Then we swept forward and were met by a terrific
fire from the enemy, so deadly that our little band was almost anni-
hilated. At this moment I ran forward waving the flag and rushed
on toward the fort. A canister struck the staff a few inches above

" ' "It's a dangerous job, my boy, to try to put that flag on that fort." ' "
—Chromolithograph, L. Prang and Co., 1888, after a painting by Thure
de Thulstrup now hanging in the 7th Regiment Armory, New York City
(LIBRARY OF CONGRESS)

my hand and cut it half in two. Then they depressed their guns and a cannonball struck the folds and carried it half away, knocking it out of my hands. I got down off the fort, picked up the flag and, rushing back, flaunted it in the faces of the Rebels and said: 'What flag are you fighting under today, Johnny?' The reply to my question was: 'You'd better surrender, Yank.' 'Oh no, Johnny, you'll surrender first,' was my answer.

"Only three of my comrades succeeded in reaching the fort with me: Sergeant Nagle, who was killed on the spot, and a private from the 54th Ohio who shared the same fate. I never left that place of death until after midnight. My canteen was shot away, my clothes were full of holes, and the banner was hardly recognizable. Then I crawled back over the corpses of the 'forlorn hope,' over dead and dying, through the cane, and back into our lines with the remnant of the flag."

A HERO

At Austerlitz and Waterloo
    Brave men each column led,
Great patriots fought, the brave and true,
    Ten thousand heroes bled!
At Lexington and Bunker Hill
    Our patriots led the van,
They fought for right with ready will
    For God and native land.

Of one brave boy let poets sing
    Throughout the land at large,
The boy who made the welkin ring,
    At Vicksburg's fearful charge.
He led a thousand men that day
    Up to the fortress high,
The Stars and Stripes he did display,
    He let his colors fly.

We stormed the works upon the north,
    Hot shell flew from the south,
When fearless Trogden with his flag,
    Rushed to the cannon's mouth.
Our dead were scattered o'er the field.
    "Fall back!" a voice did cry,
But Trogden said "I'll never yield,
    I'll plant this flag or die."

Upon the works we see him now,
    His flag still in its place,
He has kept his word, his sacred vow,
    And shook it in their face.
He drew the fire from every side—
    They let their bullets fly—
When Pemberton then loudly cried:
    "He is too brave to die."

All day he stood upon that ground
    With flagstaff in his hand;

Where can so brave a man be found
　Throughout this mighty land.

When this gigantic war is o'er,
　And treason finds its grave,
When we go home to fight no more,
　We'll not forget the brave.
And when our boys are old and gray,
　And live in quiet rest,
May Howell Trogden see that day
　With wife and children blest.

And when within his own dear home,
　His friends and neighbors are,
He'll tell them how he used to roam
　When scouting in the war.
And may his trembling hand unroll
　That same Red, White and Blue—
That flag he values more than gold—
　And waved the conflict through.

X

Gettysburg

THE town of Gettysburg, Pennsylvania, was the scene of the greatest battle ever fought on the American continent. The Union forces engaged in this renowned three-day struggle numbered about 85,000 men, whereas the Confederates had between 70,000 and 75,000 men on the field. Each army suffered over 25 per cent casualties: the Union losses were more than 23,000 killed, wounded, captured and missing; the Confederates sustained over 20,000 casualties.

The climax of the battle came on the third day when General Lee launched Pickett's Charge directly toward the center of the Union line. By today's standards, Brigadier General Lewis A. Armistead, who led the spearhead of that assault, with his hat on the point of his sword, and Lieutenant Alonzo H. Cushing, who fired the last shot from the last gun of Battery A, 4th U.S. Artillery, would both have received the Medal of Honor. They fell within twenty feet of each other, but General Armistead was in the Confederate States Army which had no Medal of Honor.

If the awarding of posthumous decorations had been customary in the Civil War, the name of Lieutenant Alonzo H. Cushing would have been included on the list of those receiving the nation's highest award. And, if the U.S. Navy had seen fit to give the Medal of Honor to officers during the war, the name Cushing would have appeared twice on those lists. His younger brother, Lieutenant William B. Cushing, U.S.N., would have been awarded the Navy Medal for the destruction of the Confederate ram *Albemarle* on October 27, 1864. It would seem that what Admiral Porter said of the younger brother would apply to both, for displaying heroism, "seldom equalled and never excelled."

Accounts of the Battle of Gettysburg tend to emphasize the third day, July 3, but the best letters in the Kohen collection came from men who won the medal on either July 1 or July 2, 1863, when it appeared as if the Confederates were going to win the battle.

Major Sellers wrote a long letter, giving the highlight of his army service throughout the war:

"Alfred J. Sellers was born March 2, 1836, in Plumsteadville, Bucks County, Pennsylvania. At the age of twenty-five he was commissioned a captain in Company B, 19th Pennsylvania Volunteers, Colonel Peter Lyle commanding. On the 18th day of April, in response to the first call of the President for volunteers, the regiment was accepted and proceeded to Locust Point, Maryland. His company was assigned to special duty to and from Washington, and was mustered out August 9, 1861, upon expiration of term of service. The regiment was reorganized for three years' service as the 90th Pennsylvania Volunteers; Captain Sellers was commissioned major. . . .

"At the Battle of Antietam . . . he was selected to command the skirmish line of the First Corps on the morning succeeding the general battle. When the fight was expected to be renewed, Major Sellers advanced his line at the first dawn of day, only to be resisted by a rear guard left to make a demonstration to give time to Lee's forces to cross the Potomac, which was chiefly accomplished during the night. The first information of Lee's retreat was forwarded by Major Sellers to General McClellan, in the absence of paper, upon a shingle, properly endorsed through intermediate headquarters. One hundred and twenty-five prisoners were captured by the skirmish line under Major Sellers, and a number were killed and wounded in driving back the rear guard.

"On the morning succeeding the Battle of Chantilly, Virginia, while in command of the skirmish line, Major Sellers received the remains of that gallant patriot, Major General Philip Kearny, under a flag of truce. General Lee's Adjutant General, Colonel Taylor, accompanied the remains. At the Battle of Fredericksburg, December 13, 1862, Major Sellers was wounded in the leg, and it is remarkable to relate that every major in this battle was either killed or wounded. After an absence of three months, he rejoined his regiment in time for the next engagement at Chancellorsville.

"At the Battle of Gettysburg, he succeeded to command of the regiment, Colonel Lyle having been assigned to the command of the brigade. It was in this battle that he won his Congressional Medal of Honor by superintending a change of front under an enfilading fire. Celerity of action was requisite, for the quicker the new position was attained the greater the saving of life and limb to us, and directly opposite results to our advancing foe. The regiment held the Post of Honor—it being on the extreme right of the First Corps—and, to protect its flank, had to refuse the line of battle and form an angle obtuse in character. . . .

"The order awarding the medal was in the following language: 'This officer, not being in command of his regiment, voluntarily rushed to the front under a withering fire and, inspiring the men by the courage of his example, led the regiment to a position from which the assault was repulsed.'

"Soon after the Gettysburg Campaign a lull in army movements was prevalent, owing to the prostrate condition of both armies. Orders from the War Department were issued detailing three officers and eight noncommissioned officers from among those most deserving during the campaign, to report to their respective homes for draft service. Major Sellers was detailed and, on July 31, 1863, was assigned to duty at Camp Cadwalader, Philadelphia, as an Instructor of Tactics.

"The first replacement detachment to the Army of the Potomac was forwarded under the command of Major Sellers, chiefly substitutes representing almost every nationality. While enroute through the Chesapeake Canal, an attempt was made on the boat to overpower the guard and escape. The ringleader, a notorious prize fighter named Price, while attempting an assault, was instantly killed which alone was the means of suppressing an organized attempt to escape.

"Major Sellers reported to the front with every man of his detachment, numbering nigh two hundred. He was court-martialed for the shooting, honorably acquitted, and received the approbation of the general commanding the department, Major General John P. Hatch, and a letter of commendation for his efficiency while under his command.

"After participating in the Mine Run Campaign, he remained in command of his regiment until December 19, 1863, when Colonel Lyle, who had been for sometime in command of the brigade, resumed command of the regiment. . . .

"On July 2, 1864, he was assigned to duty in the Shenandoah Valley in charge of supply trains. He participated in one of the most brilliant battles of the war, Cedar Creek, Virginia, as Volunteer Aide to General Dwight, 1st Division, 19th Army Corps, and was especially commended in writing, and subsequently was assigned to duty on his staff.

"After Sheridan's success in clearing the valley of Jubal Early, a new base of supplies was created. All the trains were sent to Washington under the direction of Major Sellers when, on May 19, 1865, he was assigned as Chief Quartermaster, Defenses of Washington, under General M. D. Hardin, who was succeeded by General Haskin in July 1865.

"At Washington a board was created for the examination of officers desiring to remain in the service. On August 15, 1865, Major Sellers passed the examination, was reported qualified, but declined assignment to the Department of the South. . . . On October 31, 1865, he was mustered out of the service, after having served four years, one month and twenty-one days."

The town of Gettysburg and the family name of Roosevelt are both famous in American history although the two are not generally associated. On one occasion they were brought together via the Kohen collection.

President Franklin Delano Roosevelt was an avid stamp collector and on several occasions dropped in to Charlie Kohen's shop. On one of the President's visits the collection of letters from Medal of Honor winners was mentioned; Charlie told F. D. R. that there was a letter in the collection from a Roosevelt.

A few days later the President asked to see the letter. As Charlie recalls the interview that followed, he never intended to give the letter to the President, only to show it to him. They were both hanging on to the piece of paper and the President was saying: "And here, for years, I was brought up on the story that Teddy Roosevelt was the hero of the family. Now I find that it was my own third cousin."

F. D. R. wasn't about to let go of the paper. Charlie saw that if he didn't let go of it, the letter would be torn. At this point, Charlie had no choice but to say, "My compliments, Mr. President."

Later the White House sent photostats and it is from these photostats that the following is taken:

"75. Boulevard de Waterloo,
Brussels, Belgium
January 9, 1894

My dear Sir and Comrade:

I have pleasure in acknowledging receipt of your favor of December 23, 1893, and in filling out the blank as requested. I may mention that at the time of action (Bull Run) which won for me my medal, I was only 19 years of age, having enlisted at the early age of seventeen. I inclose herewith a photograph taken two years ago. Please tell me the cost of your book when it is finished.

Very sincerely yours,
Geo. W. Roosevelt
U.S. Consul"

At this point it is necessary to refer to the form which George W. Roosevelt completed for Mr. Otis, and also to the War Department citation. Although only one Medal of Honor was issued, First Sergeant George W. Roosevelt, Company K, 26th Pennsylvania Infantry, from Chester, Pennsylvania, was cited twice—at the Second Battle of Bull Run, August 30, 1862, and at Gettysburg, July 2, 1863.

The first part of the citation reads: "At Bull Run, Va., recaptured the colors, which had been seized by the enemy." Apparently Roosevelt considered this as the more important of the two because his letter, quoted above, refers to this action only. However, the events that occurred at Gettysburg cannot be overlooked for, as Roosevelt wrote on his form, "Lost my left leg at Gettysburg." The second part of the War Department citation reads: "At Gettysburg captured a Confederate color bearer and color, in which effort he was severely wounded." George Roosevelt's explanation is a little more specific: "Captured a Rebel flag at Gettysburg, Pennsylvania (but was wounded before I could get away with it)." He added that, for wounds received and gallant and meritorious conduct at Gettysburg, he was commissioned a brevet captain of Pennsylvania Infantry Volunteers by the governor of the state.

Gettysburg was a series of crises. Of these, the struggle for possession of the Round Tops was perhaps the most critical of them all. If, on the afternoon of July 2, 1863, a less capable officer had been in command of the 20th Maine, the Battle of Gettysburg would probably have been a southern victory. Of all the Congres-

" 'Captured a Rebel flag at Gettysburg, Pennsylvania (but was wounded before I could get away with it).' "—For gallant and meritorious conduct, First Sergeant George W. Roosevelt was commissioned a brevet captain of Pennsylvania Volunteers.
(WASHINGTON POST)

"Gettysburg was a series of crises. Of these, the struggle for possession of the Round Tops was perhaps the most critical of them all."—Oil painting by Edwin Forbes of the attack on Little Round Top, July 2, 1863
(LIBRARY OF CONGRESS)

"If, on the afternoon of July 2, 1863, a less capable officer had been in command of the 20th Maine, the Battle of Gettysburg would probably have been a southern victory."—Joshua L. Chamberlain as a brigadier general

sional Medals of Honor awarded in the history of our country, that won by Joshua L. Chamberlain is particularly outstanding. It is not surprising that in later years the people elected him governor of the state of Maine, although he made no mention of this in his letter.

"All the questions on your sheet appear to have been answered except that calling for a sketch of the service for which this medal was given.

"This, I hardly know how to answer. Such recognitions are supposed to be given after investigation of the facts by the authorities of the Government, upon the testimony of some competent and credible witness, presumably a superior commanding officer. In my own case such testimony was laid before the Government by General A. S. Webb, Chief of Staff to General Meade commanding the Army of the Potomac. General Webb sent me a copy of the paper he had sent, but I cannot now put my hand on it. It is of as much value to me as the medal itself because it is an official recognition, unbiased by any after, or sinister influence. Among the testimony which was in the hands of the War Department, and which no doubt was the basis of the action taken in my case, was the following from my immediate commander at Gettysburg, General James C. Rice. He says:

" 'At the Battle of Gettysburg, Colonel Chamberlain held the extreme left of our entire line of battle. For the brilliant success of the second day's struggle, history will give credit to the bravery and unflinching fortitude of his regiment more than to any equal body of men upon the field—conduct, which as an eyewitness, I do not hesitate to say, had its inspiration and great success from the moral power and personal heroism of Colonel Chamberlain. Promotion is but a partial reward for his magnificent gallantry on the hard-won field of Gettysburg.'

"This seems rather warm language for an official paper but something not unlike it was said by all my commanders in successive order. What led to this I hardly know. It seems to me I did no more than should have been expected of me, and what it was my duty to do under the sudden and great responsibilities which fell upon me there.

"The facts were that, being ordered to hold that ground—the extreme left flank of the Union position—and finding myself unable to hold it by the mere defensive, after more than a third of my men had fallen, and my ammunition was exhausted, as well as all we could snatch from the cartridge boxes of the fallen—friend and foe—upon the field, and having at that moment right upon me a third desperate onset of the enemy with more than three times my numbers, I saw no way to hold the position but to make a counter-charge with the bayonet, and to place myself at the head of it. It happened that we were successful. We cleared the enemy entirely away from the left flank of our lines, extended and secured the commanding heights still to our left, and brought back from our charge twice as many prisoners as the entire number of men in our own ranks.

"The promotion recommended by my superior officers did not follow. I was without political influence in Washington, without which, in those days, no military merit in the field could claim attention among the many nearer interests that pressed upon the Government. But, in a month from that battle, my military superiors had advanced me to the command of a brigade, although the Government had not conferred on me that rank.

"It was not until after General Grant had promoted me on the field of battle, and I had been made a major general by brevet 'for conspicuous gallantry' in the first battle of the last campaign, and had been designated to command the parade at the surrender of Lee's Army at Appomattox Court House, and had received mention for the Medal of Honor on two occasions (The White Oak Road and Appomattox Court House), that this incident of Gettysburg came up again. All the cases were laid before the Government but, as the Battle of Gettysburg was the most famous one, my recommender chose this.

"I ask pardon for so many words but your questions seemed to require me to tell you what I could about the matter. It certainly needed some explanation. I do not see what you could say in a few words except perhaps: 'for repelling an overpowering assault, with a bayonet countercharge, led by him in person.' For I remember that, as we struck the enemy's onrushing lines, I was confronted by an officer, also in front of his line, who fired one shot of his revolver at my head within six feet of me. When, in an instant, the point of my sabre was at his throat, he quickly presented me with both his pistol and his sword, which I have preserved as memorials of my narrow escape."

X I

Negro Troops at Chaffin's Farm

WHEN people think of bravery in battle, their thoughts almost automatically turn first to the big battles with the famous names. It is natural to assume that the majority of the medals for valor, awarded by a grateful government, were earned on those battlefields with the well-known names. And whenever the part played by Negroes in the Civil War is mentioned, two major events immediately come to mind: the celebrated attack on Fort Wagner, South Carolina, and the Battle of the Crater at Petersburg, Virginia. A student of the war might well assume that the majority of the Army's Medals of Honor issued to Negroes were awarded for gallantry in those two assaults, but the student would be wrong in his assumption. There were sixteen Army Congressional Medals of Honor issued to colored troops for valor during the Civil War, but the majority were won on another field on another day.

Likewise, a student of the war might assume that at least one-half of the medals awarded by the Navy Department to Negroes would have been won by men who served on ships with famous names. In this case, the student would be right. There were four medals issued to Negro sailors, and two of them went to men for bravery in action on two of the best-known ships in the United States Navy—U.S.S. *Hartford* and U.S.S. *Kearsarge*.

The first Negro to perform an heroic deed, for which the Congressional Medal of Honor was later awarded, was Sergeant William H. Carney, Company C, 54th Massachusetts Colored Infantry. The date was July 18, 1863, which means that the occasion was the gallant but unsuccessful assault on Fort Wagner, the strongest fortification on Morris Island, protecting the harbor of Charleston, South Carolina. History records that the attack failed, but history also tells of the bravery of the men of the 54th Massachusetts who led the charge. One could wish that the War Department's citations

"The first Negro to perform an heroic deed, for which the Congressional Medal of Honor was later awarded, was Sergeant William H. Carney, Company C, 54th Massachusetts Colored Infantry."—Photo taken several years after the war

in the Civil War period were more informative. Usually they were far too brief but the one for Sergeant Carney of New Bedford, Massachusetts, is more descriptive than most. It gives at least a fair idea of what he endured: "When the color sergeant was shot down, this soldier grasped the flag, led the way to the parapet, and planted the colors thereon. When the troops fell back he brought off the flag, under a fierce fire in which he was twice severely wounded."

Sergeant Carney, like so many other soldiers in the Army, did not receive the Medal of Honor until long after the war was over. The first Negro actually to receive the medal was a former slave who had escaped and was serving on the U.S. Steam Gunboat *Marblehead.* On Christmas Day, 1863, Confederate batteries opened an early morning attack on his ship in the Stono River near Legare-ville, nine miles south of Charleston. The duel lasted more than an hour until the Confederates withdrew. For outstanding gallantry in this engagement, Robert Blake became the first Negro to receive the Navy Medal of Honor. He was cited in Navy Department General Order 32, issued April 16, 1864: "Serving the rifle gun, Blake, an escaped slave, carried out his duties bravely throughout the engagement which resulted in the enemy's abandonment of positions, leaving a caisson and one gun behind."

The next general order awarding a Medal of Honor to a Negro was issued on the last day of the year, December 31, 1864. General Order Number 45, however, contained the names of not one, but two Negroes, who were cited for gallantry on two very famous naval vessels.

The most renowned single ship actions of the Civil War were the clash between the steam-powered ironclads *Merrimac* and *Monitor* on March 9, 1862; and the duel off the coast of France between the U.S.S. *Kearsarge* and the most feared sea raider of them all, the Confederate cruiser *Alabama.* It was in the second of these two battles that Seaman Joachim Pease performed the outstanding service for which he was cited in general orders. Unfortunately neither Joachim Pease nor any of the other Negroes who won the Navy Medal of Honor wrote to James Otis to describe how they earned their medals. However, the Navy Department's general orders were, in most cases, issued soon after the event and generally gave more information than the awards in the Army Medal of Honor book. In the case of Joachim Pease, the Navy said: "Served as seaman on board the U.S.S. *Kearsarge* when she destroyed the *Alabama* off Cherbourg, France, 19 June 1864. Acting as loader on the No. 2 gun during this bitter engagement, Pease exhibited marked coolness and good conduct and was highly recommended by his divisional officer for gallantry under fire."

In the same Navy general order, John Lawson was named and a Medal of Honor awarded to him for his part in the most important naval battle of the war, the Battle of Mobile Bay, August 5, 1864, forever famous in naval tradition for Admiral David G. Farragut's: "Damn the torpedoes. Go ahead." John Lawson was serving on the flagship U.S.S. *Hartford*: "Wounded in the leg and thrown violently against the side of the ship when an enemy shell killed or wounded the six-man crew at the shell whip on the berth deck, Lawson, upon regaining his composure, promptly returned to his station and, although urged to go below for treatment, steadfastly continued his duties throughout the remainder of the action."

The fourth and last Negro to win the Navy Medal had a most unusual experience. Aaron Anderson was a member of a boat crew engaged in attempting to clear a creek when his boat came under "a devastating fire which cut away half the oars, pierced the launch in many places and cut the barrel off a musket being fired at the enemy." One wonders how any of the boat crew escaped unless the Confederate snipers magnanimously let them go. The date was March 17, 1865, and the war was almost over.

Only one of the sixteen Army Medals of Honor awarded to Negro soldiers has been mentioned. In July, 1864, two other Negroes performed deeds of courage on the battlefield which were later recognized. Sergeant Major Thomas Hawkins, 6th United States Colored Troops, was awarded the medal for the rescue of his regimental colors at Deep Bottom, Virginia, on July 21, 1864. The Army Medal of Honor book is disappointingly brief in his case but, for Sergeant Decatur Dorsey, Company B, 39th United States Colored Troops, the record is more satisfactory.

The occasion was the Battle of the Crater. A tunnel over 500 feet long had been dug under the Confederate entrenchments protecting Petersburg. At 4:45 A.M., July 30, 1864, over four tons of powder were exploded, blowing a huge crater in the Confederate lines. A Union division rushed into the gap but, instead of pressing forward to pursue their advantage, most of the personnel stayed in the crater. Two more divisions advanced; later they were joined by a colored division. By this time, however, the defenders had been given a chance to recover from the shock of the explosion. Confederate artillery fire was poured into the thousands of men jammed together in that crowded space. A Confederate counterattack then restored the lines. The failure on the part of the leading units to

advance had converted a splendid opportunity into a gloomy failure, which was relieved only by brave exploits of individuals such as Sergeant Dorsey, whose official participation was described thus: "Planted his colors on the Confederate works in advance of his regiment, and when the regiment was driven back to the Union works he carried the colors there and bravely rallied the men."

The other thirteen Army Medals were all awarded for bravery in a battle which never became well known to the general public, although the army commander did his best to publicize it. Unfortunately for the troops concerned the army commander was Major General Benjamin F. "Beast" Butler, who was surely one of the worst officers ever to wear the uniform of a general in the United States Army. At the beginning of the war President Lincoln had been forced, for political reasons, to appoint a number of prominent persons, with great influence, to positions of high command in the Army. Some of them proved to be very capable officers. Others, however, caused the President a tremendous amount of embarrassment. In the long run their appointments caused far more harm than good, yet it was still difficult to get rid of them because they retained a great

The Confederate counterattack at the Battle of the Crater, July 30, 1864—From the painting in the Commonwealth Club, Richmond, Virginia
(LIBRARY OF CONGRESS)

deal of political influence. Of all those in this second category Benjamin F. Butler was probably the worst.

In the year 1864, Butler was in command of the Army of the James in Southeast Virginia. He had been originally ordered to attack Richmond from the southeast while the main army, the Army of the Potomac, advanced from the north against General Lee's army. Butler had failed miserably in this effort and, in later attacks directed toward the capture of Petersburg, had contributed materially toward failure there also. As a result, both President Lincoln and General Grant had grown to distrust almost everything having to do with Butler. Both of them would have been most happy to rid themselves of him but, up to that time, there had always been extenuating circumstances, so that the case against Butler had not been sufficiently clear-cut to dispose of such a prominent politician. Eventually, in January, 1865, after Butler's abysmal failure in the attack on Fort Fisher, North Carolina, in December, 1864, political necessity was ignored; Grant recommended and Lincoln approved Butler's removal from command.

All of this was most unfortunate for any troops, white or colored, who had the misfortune to serve under Butler. He would issue bombastic proclamations announcing how much he and the men of his command had accomplished. Naturally his soldiers tended to believe his exaggerated claims but others who had learned to take almost all his statements with several grains of salt were not inclined to place too much credence in his reports. By 1864, Ben Butler's reputation for truth and veracity was not too high; the reputation of the troops under his command suffered in consequence.

It is difficult to determine how much is true and how much is false whenever Butler's reports are compared with the reports of other officers. The engagement in which thirteen Negroes won the Medal of Honor on September 29 and 30, 1864, is no exception. It does not help matters either to discover that a large number of the commanders involved in the action did not submit any reports. And, to make matters more confusing, this engagement has been referred to in various places by different names. The official records of the war refer to the battle as Chaffin's Farm, but the Army Medal of Honor book calls it Chapins Farm, and one of the medals was issued for gallantry at New Market Heights. The use of this name New Market is particularly disconcerting because it is almost sure to become confused with the famous battle of that name fought in the Shenandoah Valley on May 15, 1864, four and one-half months before Chaffin's Farm.

Students of the war will, however, recognize the action readily if they are told that the Battle of Chaffin's Farm refers to the Union attack launched against Fort Gilmer, and that it was delivered on the same day as the successful Union assault on Fort Harrison just north of the James River. The latter was only lightly defended and was easily captured by the 1st Division of the Eighteenth Corps; Confederate efforts to retake it on the 30th of September failed.

Fort Gilmer, next in line to Fort Harrison, was more strongly held. The advanced line of entrenchments was seized, but Confederate reinforcements arrived in time. Then, the main line withstood all attacks delivered by the remainder of the troops present from both the Tenth and Eighteenth Corps. On this occasion Butler's proclamation gave the impression that every assault undertaken by the troops under his command succeeded gloriously. If such had been the case, his army would have swept onward almost to Richmond. Since this did not happen, Butler's claims were generally shrugged away as being preposterous as usual, and the troops never received due credit for what they accomplished, bravely, and at great cost to themselves. The Medals of Honor issued for these dates to colored troops were all awarded to men of the 2nd and 3rd Brigades of the 3rd Division, Eighteenth Corps. Nine of the medals went to men of the 2nd. Brigade; four were issued to men of the 3rd Brigade.

Sergeant Major Christian A. Fleetwood who enlisted at Baltimore, Maryland, and later after the war, moved to Washington, D.C., did not write a long letter to describe what he did to win his medal. However, his description was truly representative of all four of the medals awarded to men in the 3rd Brigade, three in his regiment and one in another regiment. In every one of these four cases, involving two different regiments, the medals were awarded for bravery in saving the colors. Sergeant Major Fleetwood of the 4th United States Colored Troops apparently saw no necessity to give a vivid description; the casualty figures spoke for him: "Saved the regimental colors after eleven of the twelve color guards had been shot down around it."

A long letter came from a member of the 2nd Brigade, 3rd Division, Eighteenth Corps. By coincidence, Milton M. Holland, 5th United States Colored Troops, had also been a sergeant major, the highest rank that a Negro could then officially attain in the United States Army.

The letter gives an account of his entire service but, in describing the action at Chaffin's Farm, it is not too specific as to his own part. Milton Holland preferred to dwell instead upon the valor of the entire regiment. His personal citation was for taking command of Company C, and gallantly leading it after all the officers had been killed or wounded.

"Milton M. Holland was born in the state of Texas in 1844. He was attending school in Athens County, Ohio, in 1861 when the first call was made for volunteer soldiers, and was among the first boys of his school to throw down his books and respond to the call of his country. He enlisted in the Union Army in April, 1861, but was rejected on account of his youth. But so determined was he to serve his country that he immediately sought employment in the Quartermaster Department and served under Colonel Nelson H. Van Vorhis of the 3rd, 18th and 92nd Ohio Volunteer Infantry.

"'Saved the regimental colors after eleven of the twelve color guards had been shot down around it.'"—Sergeant Major Christian A. Fleetwood
(MANUSCRIPT DIVISION, LIBRARY OF CONGRESS)

"His personal citation was for taking command of Company C, and gallantly leading it after all the officers had been killed or wounded."—Newspaper sketch of Milton M. Holland
(KOHEN COLLECTION)

"He served in this capacity until he was regularly mustered into the Union Army in June, 1863 and assigned to the 5th United States Colored Troops, a regiment raised in Ohio and accredited to that state. With his regiment he engaged in the campaigns in Virginia and North Carolina under the command of General B. F. Butler. In the winter of 1863 he was with his regiment in the raid through the Dismal Swamp into North Carolina, capturing forage and emancipating slaves under the then recent Emancipation Proclamation.

"In the early winter and spring of 1864, he was with his regiment in the two raids from Yorktown, Virginia to Bottom's Bridge just outside Richmond: the first raid being made for the purpose of liberating the Union prisoners confined at Libby Prison; and the second for the purpose of assisting General Kilpatrick who, in his attempt to relieve the Libby Prison men, had been surrounded by the Confederate forces.

"He was with the James River fleet in its advance on Richmond and, as the fleet approached City Point, Company C, of which Holland was then the 1st Sergeant, was ordered to make the attack. The order was promptly obeyed and, without landing the vessel, the men jumped from the guard rail of the boat, wading water waist deep to reach the point of attack. They captured the Rebel flag, the signal station and signal officers of the Confederacy, and thus struck the first signal blow at the Rebel stronghold at Petersburg.

"This regiment was part of the famous Black Brigade which General Smith at first refused to use in his charge on Petersburg on June 15, 1864. General Butler, commanding the corps, promptly ordered General Smith to march on Petersburg and storm her breastworks. General Smith led the black phalanx in the charge and, for the courage, the heroism, the daring and skill displayed by the colored troops in that bloody fight, General Smith remarked that he would lead men like those into any fight and rely upon their pluck.

"His regiment was at the 'Mine Explosion' on July 30, and was prepared to make the charge. They received instructions at a given signal to discharge their guns onto the enemy's line, jump the parapet and ditch, and make a charge to cover the 'Crater.' But just before the signal was given it was discovered that another division was substituted in their place. This circumstance, young Holland has ever maintained, lost a day to the Union forces that otherwise would have been gained. It was at this battle that Holland had planned and decided to cover himself all over with glory. He was sorely disappointed but never relinquished the desire and intention to avail himself of the first opportunity.

"In the latter part of August, 1864, his regiment moved to the right in front of Richmond at Deep Bottom. It was at this point that his regiment made its brilliant and famous charge on the 29th day of September, 1864. And it was there that Sergeant Major Holland led the assaulting company of his regiment in their famous charge. Brilliant as had been its past record, and courageous as the men had shown themselves to be on other fields, this one occasion seems to have been reserved as the crucial test of their fighting qualities. When they met the enemy, they fought hand to hand with a desperate valor that beggared description. The shot and shell of the enemy mowed down the front ranks of the colored troops like blades of grass beneath the sickle's deadly touch. But, with a courage that knew no bounds, the men stood like granite figures. They routed the enemy and captured the breastworks. The courage displayed by young Holland's regiment on this occasion called for the highest praise from General Grant who personally rode over the battlefield in company with Generals Butler and Draper. . . .

"Holland was wounded in this battle but did not leave the field. Later in the day the regiment made a charge at Fort Harrison to relieve a brigade of white troops that was unable to get back to the Union lines.

" 'The courage displayed by young Holland's regiment on this occasion called for the highest praise from General Grant . . .' "—Woodcut from a drawing by F. B. Schell of the Battle of Chaffin's Farm, September 29, 1864

(LIBRARY OF CONGRESS)

"Immediately after the charge at New Market Heights, Holland was examined on the field by order of General Butler and passed for captain, but was, on account of color, refused his commission by the War Department. Twice he was presented with medals which were awarded him for bravery and distinguished services on the field of battle. One of these medals was voted him by Congress and forwarded to him through President Lincoln, and the other was awarded by General B. F. Butler.

"He served with his regiment at Dutch Gap until October 4th, when the regiment went over to Fair Oaks, or Seven Pines, where the Union forces achieved a victory of which they were afterwards deprived by a successful ruse of the enemy.

"In December, 1864, the regiment went with the great naval fleet under General Butler to Fortress Fisher at the mouth of the Cape Fear River in an attempt to break up the blockade-running at that point. Although Holland's regiment landed at Fortress Fisher, they were compelled to withdraw on account of the insufficiency of support. But they returned in January, 1865, under command of General Terry when this fort was captured.

"He was with his regiment on its marches through Wilmington, Bentonville, Goldsboro, and Raleigh. He was present when General Joseph E. Johnston surrendered to General W. T. Sherman, and it was here that his regiment received the sad tidings of the death of President Lincoln, when men of iron nerves shed tears like broken-hearted children."

XII

Our Immigrant Heroes

"All of our people—except full-blooded Indians—are immigrants, or descendants of immigrants, including even those who came here on the Mayflower.*"*
—Franklin Delano Roosevelt, Boston, November 4, 1944

IN THE thirty years immediately preceding the Civil War there was a great flood of immigrants to the United States from Europe, principally from Ireland and Germany. In the decade from 1840 to 1850 almost one and a half million people came to this country. By 1860 nearly one-seventh of the total population consisted of persons who had been born abroad, and by far the greater number of these people settled in the industrial North rather than in the agricultural South.

During the war years, from 1861 to 1865, there was a very large peace party in the North opposed to the war. It might be supposed that these were the immigrants, but the exact opposite was generally true. The immigrants, many of whom had come from countries where they had been exposed to warfare in one form or another for countless generations, accepted the war for the Union with few questions asked. They had come here to live; they had no traditions of states' rights; this was their new country and they were prepared to fight for it. The rolls of the Congressional Medal of Honor contain numerous names of men born in Ireland or Germany. Several who answered James Otis' letters came from England. Others who wrote, and whose answers are recorded in this chapter, or elsewhere in this book, came from Scotland, Wales, Belgium, France, Norway, Hungary, and other places.

Prominent among the stream of immigrants from Europe to America were the Jews. During the Napoleonic era the Jewish people had been treated with much greater consideration than previously. However, Napoleon's liberalism had been followed, in many places, by restoration of all the old discriminations.

Leopold Karpeles, born in Prague in 1838, was probably typical of the many thousands who left Europe in the 1840's to seek greater freedom from persecution and discrimination. At the age of eleven he left for America to live with an older brother who had settled several years earlier in Galveston, Texas. However, before the outbreak of the war, he had moved to Springfield, Massachusetts, where he enlisted in September 1862 in Company A of the 46th Massachusetts Volunteers. When he was mustered out, his officers testified to the courageous manner in which he carried the colors of his regiment in several battles fought in North Carolina.

In March 1864, Karpeles reenlisted in Company E, 57th Massachusetts Volunteers. Perhaps the testimonials he had received for his prior service influenced his assignment in his new regiment, for he was selected as the color sergeant. It would appear that whenever Karpeles participated in a battle, with either of the two regiments with which he served, he invariably was chosen for this honorable but highly dangerous assignment. Yet, in recording his wartime service, he made no mention of this fact: "I participated in the following engagements: Kingston, Whitehall, Goldsborough, Gum Swamp, all in North Carolina; Wilderness, Spotsylvania, North Anna, Popular Spring Church, Hatcher's Run, all in Virginia."

It was in the Battle of the Wilderness that Karpeles performed the heroic deeds for which he was later awarded the Medal of Honor. His regiment was assigned to the 1st Brigade, 1st Division, 9th Army Corps, whose commander was Major General Ambrose E. Burnside. The corps, at this time, was not a part of the Union Army of the Potomac but operated under the direct orders of Lieutenant General Ulysses S. Grant. It was initially employed to guard the railroads but, when battle became imminent, three of its four divisions were ordered forward by forced marches. They entered the battle on the second day.

The two-day Battle of the Wilderness, fought in terribly difficult, tangled terrain, was a very confusing ordeal for both sides, punctuated by a series of assaults wherein neither army gained a distinct advantage. Karpeles' description of his part in that battle gives an excellent idea of the sort of fighting that occurred.

"I received my Medal of Honor as color sergeant in the 57th Regiment Massachusetts Volunteers. It was during the Battle of the Wilderness on May 6, 1864. When a general stampede occurred, I was the only color sergeant to stand the ground during the evening of the 6th. With the assistance of some officers, we succeeded in rallying around my colors a sufficient number of men to keep the Rebels in check, and prevented the capture of the stragglers in

"'. . . We succeeded in rallying around my colors a sufficient number of men to keep the Rebels in check . . .'"
—Leopold Karpeles, photo taken several years later, when he was active in the affairs of the Grand Army of the Republic
(COURTESY B'NAI B'RITH)

the woods. Our small body of men succeeded in holding them until after dark. Then we fell back and reorganized regiments and corps."

In his letter Leopold Karpeles also briefly described his final appearance on a battlefield, when he again carried the colors in an attack against the enemy. "I fell exhausted from the loss of blood from my wound and was paralyzed. I was unconscious for several days. When I came to, I found myself lying in a cavalry camp. From there I was sent to the hospital."

Also on May 6, 1864, in the 2nd Brigade, 2nd Division, of the same 9th Army Corps there was another Jewish immigrant due to be awarded the Medal of Honor for gallantry in action. Abraham Cohn, born in Prussia, was sergeant major of the 6th New Hampshire Infantry. His War Department citation for this action is remarkably similar to that of Karpeles. "During Battle of the Wilderness rallied and formed, under heavy fire, disorganized and fleeing troops of different regiments."

However, this is only the first part of Cohn's Medal of Honor record. He was again cited at Petersburg on July 30, 1864, on the memorable day of the Battle of the Crater. On that occasion the Army Medal of Honor book records that Sergeant Major Abraham Cohn: "bravely and coolly carried orders to the advanced line under severe fire."

This double citation was not the only one issued to a Jewish immigrant from Prussia. In 1879 the War Department awarded the Congressional Medal of Honor to David Orbansky, a former private of Company B, 58th Ohio Infantry, for gallantry in actions at Shiloh, Tennessee, in 1862 and at Vicksburg, Mississippi, in 1863.

The patriotism of these immigrants, many of whom had not lived too long in the United States, was often quite simple, clear, and uncomplicated. They did their duty as they saw it, in a direct straightforward manner. An excellent example of this was a soldier named Martin Schubert who was born in Bavaria, badly wounded at Antietam, September 17, 1862, and again at Fredericksburg on December 13, 1862. The War Department citation, referring to his part in the Battle of Fredericksburg, read: "Relinquished a furlough granted for wounds, entered the battle, where he picked up the colors after several bearers had been killed or wounded, and carried them until himself again wounded." Private Martin Schubert of the 26th New York Infantry wrote that he didn't think there were many who had gone into battle with a furlough in their pockets but, "I thought that the government needed me there."

There was nothing complicated about this man's courage. He was needed, therefore he went. Another immigrant who would have understood Schubert very well, without any long discussions on the subject of patriotism, was Joseph Gion. He enlisted at Pittsburgh, Pennsylvania, and served in a New York regiment, the 74th New York Volunteers. His record states that at Chancellorsville on May 2, 1863, he: "Voluntarily and under heavy fire advanced toward the enemy's lines and secured valuable information."

Joseph Gion had died in 1888, so when a letter asking for information reached his home, the form was filled out and a reply written by a James W. Neeley, who appears to have been the family doctor. On the form Dr. Neeley recorded Gion's birthplace as France, in the year 1826, but in the letter reprinted below he refers to Joseph Gion as German. Alsace-Lorraine might be an educated guess as to Gion's birthplace. Dr. Neeley's letter is worth quoting in full:

"Mrs. Gion has handed me this request of yours, to fill in the blank form, which I enclose. She has not a picture of her husband. On one occasion some firm wrote her for a similar outline; she sent his picture, and that was the last of it, she says.

"I was acquainted with Mr. Gion for many years before his death and talked with him about the war and learned he had been awarded a medal for a certain act of bravery. He was German and it was hard to understand him but I made out that he, with some others, had been sent out as skirmishers, a small party of them. Before they were aware, they were right in among the rebels. Their action, etc., and their getting back to where our lines were stationed, was looked upon as a great act of skill and bravery for which they were voted a medal. All that were along with him had received theirs, but he had not got his, and could not tell me the reason.

"I was at that time frequently writing for him to Major J. Thomas Turner, Attorney, Washington, D.C. about a pension claim in his hands, which by the way was granted, but so small that it amounted to nothing, only $2 per month. Well, in one of my messages I told him [Major Turner] of this medal the old man spoke of, and he commenced a search, and sure enough found it, I suppose in the Department, and sent it here. This was only a few years ago, so that his medal was all these years at Washington, very likely because he did not know how to go about getting it. Mrs. Gion showed it to me a few days ago and I have written its inscription on the blank form. This is all I can give concerning this old soldier."

There were four men engaged on this reconnaissance toward the Confederate lines on May 2, 1863. The doctor was quite correct in saying that the others had received their decorations before Gion was awarded his, but there were very valid reasons why record-keeping had, on that day, become an item of very secondary importance. For it was at 5:15 P.M. on this second day of the Battle of Chancellorsville that Stonewall Jackson had launched his overpowering assault on the Union army that gave the South its greatest victory.

Two nights later, when the Union Army of the Potomac withdrew across the Rappahannock River, an Irish-born major of infantry performed a most valuable service for his new country. Darkness was falling. It was an open question whether or not the Union forces would be able to retire without suffering heavy casualties. Major St. Clair A. Mulholland, commanding the 116th Pennsylvania Infantry, a battalion of the famous Irish Brigade, was given the assignment of protecting that withdrawal. His citation from the War Department, issued in 1895, reads: "In command of the picket lines held the enemy in check all night to cover the retreat of the Army." However, the account published in the *Philadelphia Inquirer* is much more descriptive:

"That afternoon General Hooker decided to abandon Chancellorsville and recross the Rappahannock. In withdrawing the army it was desirous that General Lee should have no knowledge of the movement, and it seemed necessary that a sacrifice should be made. The intrepid Major Mulholland was sent for, and the contemplated movement explained to him. He was told that it would be necessary all night for the picket lines to maintain a heavy fire in order to detract attention from the retiring army. The pickets, he was told, would of a certainty fall into the hands of the enemy, but without any question Mulholland volunteered to take charge of the lines. General Hooker at that time recognizing Mulholland's bravery, declared that should he be taken to a Southern prison, the government should be apprized of his heroic conduct.

"Mulholland with 400 men at once took charge of the picket lines, placing a strong guard at the only entrance to the abatis, in order that the men under him have no knowledge of the fact that the army was leaving the field. All through the night Mulholland's men kept up a continuous and heavy fire, in order to create an impression that a large number of troops were taking part in the operation, and he of all the men outside the abatis was aware that but little probability of escape was likely. The enemy was held in check all through the night, and it was 7 o'clock the next morning when a mounted aide from General Hancock's staff shouted over the abatis that the army had safely crossed the river.

"Mulholland then ordered in all the picket line and with the exception of twelve men succeeded in getting them over the river. There was general surprise and congratulation at headquarters upon his escape, for it was not thought possible that the pickets could withstand the enemy. Among the men who had been on guard when they crossed the abatis and realized that the army had been withdrawn there was the utmost consternation, and they effected the crossing of the pontoon bridge as the Union engineers were tearing up the planking and a Confederate battery was smashing the boats with shells."

For the record it should be noted that after this superb demonstration of his ability St. Clair Mulholland did not remain a major very long. He was promoted rapidly and by October 1864 had attained the rank of brevet major general. During his army career this Irishman was wounded four times: at Fredericksburg in December 1862, and in 1864 at the Battle of the Wilderness on May 5, at the Po River on May 10, and at Totopotomy Creek on May 31.

General Mulholland was not the only Irish immigrant to be awarded the Congressional Medal of Honor for bravery in action while engaged in a retreat in the face of the enemy. In the latter part of May, 1862, the Union Army of the Potomac had approached to within six miles of Richmond, Virginia, and was threatening the safety of the southern capital. Although the northern troops heavily outnumbered the defenders, the Union army was divided into two parts by the Chickahominy River. Taking advantage of this fact, the Confederates, on May 31, 1862, launched an attack upon the Union corps isolated south of the river.

Reinforcements were hastily brought toward the threatened flank, among them General Phil Kearny's division of the Third Corps. The battle that followed, known as Fair Oaks or Seven Pines, was a very confused, haphazard affair for both sides. Units were intermingled, directions lost, orders issued, and then countermanded. As the lines swayed back and forth, some men fled from the field while others stubbornly held their ground. General Kearny, finding Confederate troops cutting off his line of retreat, ordered one of his regiments to turn completely about and face toward the rear to hold off the Confederate attacks.

"... the Union Army of the Potomac had approached to within six miles of Richmond ..."—Alfred R. Waud's pencil and Chinese white drawing of Fair Oaks a day or two before the battle

(LIBRARY OF CONGRESS)

For the captain commanding Company C of this regiment, the 37th New York Volunteers, there was nothing novel about being rushed hastily to a place where danger threatened. James Rowan O'Beirne had begun the war as a private in the famous 7th Regiment of New York City. In April 1861 the North had been desperately worried about the safety of Washington, D.C. Virginia was about to secede; the people of Maryland were threatening to follow suit; Washington was in imminent danger of falling into southern hands. Northern troops were hurriedly sent for to save the city. The first to arrive was the 6th Massachusetts, which was attacked en route by a mob in Baltimore. The next two regiments to reach the scene were the 7th New York and the 8th Massachusetts. They had to go the long way around by water to Annapolis thence overland to Washington, rebuilding the railroad as they went. Thereafter Baltimore was occupied and Maryland was forced, by the presence of Union troops, to remain loyal to the Union.

Thus Captain O'Beirne, who was very proud of the part he had taken in saving the city of Washington from possible capture by the enemy, was now, one year later, faced with a much greater danger of capture by Confederate troops, practically within sight of the southern capital of Richmond.

"At the Battle of Fair Oaks, the 37th Regiment was hotly engaged. The horse of General Kearny was killed, and he came dismounted through the lines. Accosted by Captain James R. O'Beirne, he said to the men, and him, to get out the best way they could. . . .

"O'Beirne proceeded to withdraw his company in the direction of the plank road to the saw mill. The other left-wing companies followed, and O'Beirne thus succeeded in being the means of saving the left wing of the regiment. This was done under a heavy fire, and in imminent danger of being captured by the Rebels, who had turned the flank, and were pressing in to capture the artillery, which the 37th with other troops were supporting. The movement was executed successfully, and the regiment was saved."

The great majority of our immigrant heroes naturally served, or at least began their service, in the ranks. Very few were able to start the war with a high rank. One such was Julius H. Stahel (the "H" seems to have gotten lost some place in the Army records), who recorded on the form sent him that he had been born in Hungary in 1825, and had been a "journalist" before the war began. He listed as his first unit the 8th New York Volunteers, which he had helped to organize. He had then been commissioned as lieutenant colonel of the regiment.

Julius Stahel proudly let it be known that the 8th New York, in the First Battle of Bull Run, had "covered the retreat, repulsing the last attack of the enemy." The regiment had "remained on the battlefield until 2:00 a.m. the next day, and was the last regiment to arrive in Washington." He also added that they had brought back the regimental flag of a Massachusetts regiment and a guidon belonging to another New York regiment.

Before the year was out, he had been promoted to colonel and again to brigadier general. By now he was serving in the cavalry. His promotion to major general came in March 1863, and the date is significant. On March 9, Captain (later Colonel) John S. Mosby with twenty-nine Confederate partisans had gone through the Union lines into Fairfax, Virginia, captured a Union general named Stoughton, two other officers, thirty enlisted men and nearly sixty horses. Stahel wrote:

"The day when General Stoughton was captured at Fairfax Court House, President Lincoln sent for General Stahel and, telling him of the capture of General Stoughton and the insecure condition of our lines in front of Washington, asked him to take command in front of Washington and to report at once to General Heintzelman,

" '. . . President Lincoln sent for General Stahel and . . . asked him to take command in front of Washington . . .' "—Julius Stahel in later years
(KOHEN COLLECTION)

Department Commander. From March 13 to June 19, 1863, our lines in front of Washington, notwithstanding their great length, were not once broken through."

Admirers of John Singleton Mosby will agree that while General Stahel was in command there was no repetition of the Fairfax raid, but will also note the fact that Julius Stahel was no more successful than his predecessors, or his successors, in capturing the celebrated raider.

General Stahel's last battle was at Piedmont, Virginia, on June 5, 1864, a Union victory that resulted in the temporary capture of

Staunton and Lexington. In this battle, for which he was decorated twenty-nine years later, Stahel was severely wounded while leading a cavalry charge. The victory had a curious result. The Union forces marched toward Lynchburg and this threat caused General Lee to detach Jubal Early's corps from the Richmond area. One month later Jubal Early had crossed into Maryland and was making his famous demonstration against Washington, D.C.

Perhaps the most astounding reply that James Otis received came from Elmer I. Davis of the Adams Express Company, East Palestine, Columbiana County, Ohio. It concerned his father, Joseph Davis, who had been born in Wales on May 22, 1838. Today a letter such as this would be completely unbelievable. Alert reporters would long before have picked up the story of this presentation of an award for heroism in combat. The home-town newspapers would have publicized all the particulars in full. Yet the younger Davis' letter began:

"I enclose you a history of my father during the war and also the medal which he was awarded by the Congress. I did not know anything about the Medal, and I had to look up some of my father's comrades, and they told me about it, and this is as near as I can tell you. . . .

"I also send you a picture of my father. It is not a very good one, but it is all that I have. It was taken from a tin type which was taken before the war. . . .

"My father enlisted for the term of three years. He was promoted to corporal in the hospital at David's Island, N.Y.H. [New York

"'I did not know anything about the Medal, and I had to look up some of my father's comrades, and they told me about it . . .'" Joseph Davis did not even tell his son that he had been awarded the Medal of Honor. —The only picture the son had was "not a very good one . . . from a tin type which was taken before the war. . . ."
(KOHEN COLLECTION)

Harbor] and was discharged on the 29th of May, 1865 by individual muster out at David's Island, N.Y.H. while holding the grade of corporal.

"My father was at the Siege of Knoxville . . . and was in all the battles with the company throughout the Atlanta Campaign. The Company (C) belonged to the Army of the Ohio, 23rd Corps, 1st Brigade and 3rd Division.

"The Medal was awarded to him for the capture of a Rebel flag at the Battle of Franklin, Tennessee which was fought on the 30th of November, 1864."

It is one of the mysteries of the Civil War that the Battle of Franklin has never received the attention it deserves. Gettysburg and Pickett's Charge are household words today. Yet at Franklin more southern soldiers were in the assault. They had a greater distance to charge across the open fields. The defending Union army (unlike the army at Gettysburg) was heavily outnumbered but was sheltered by strong log and dirt entrenchments. Yet the assault broke through the center of the Union line and was stopped only by a fierce counterattack, while the troops holding the shoulders of the penetration held firm. In this charge more Confederate generals and soldiers were killed than at Gettysburg.

Despite these facts neither the men who took part in this assault nor those who so bravely repelled the attack have ever received proper acknowledgment of their deeds. If they had, it would have been entirely unnecessary for Elmer Davis to mention the name of the battle. He could have simply given the date and said that his father had fought with the 104th Ohio Volunteers on that fearful day.

From his father's comrades the son learned that "he captured the flag from the Color Bearer after a hard fight for it, and after the Rebels had charged over the Union forces' breastworks. He was wounded at the battle and was sent to the hospital."

XIII

Behind the Lines

IN THIS war, where the operations of the armies covered such an immense expanse of territory, the establishment of fixed front lines hundreds of miles long, stretching halfway across the continent, was manifestly impossible. Even in territory supposedly under the control of friendly forces it was necessary to be on guard at all times against a surprise attack.

About three weeks after the Battle of Gettysburg, while the armies were recuperating from that strenuous campaign, First Lieutenant John Wesley Clark of Montpelier, Vermont, regimental quartermaster of the 6th Vermont Volunteers, found himself in charge of a division supply train moving slowly westward toward Manassas Gap in the Blue Ridge Mountains. It was a perfectly routine march, well behind the so-called front lines, and his train guard consisted of only a small group of convalescent soldiers.

Suddenly the little supply column was attacked by a raiding force of enemy cavalry. After a brief but spirited engagement the raiders were repulsed. Lieutenant Clark was severely wounded but, according to the Army's Medal of Honor book, "remained in the saddle for 20 hours afterward, until he had brought his train through in safety."

John Wesley Clark's letter was selected for inclusion in this book not because his was a particularly outstanding act of bravery above and beyond the call of duty, nor because it is a good example of leadership and devotion to duty for which today he would have been awarded a decoration of lesser degree, but because of his tongue-in-cheek humor when he wrote of his experience.

Surely Clark knew that the lines he wrote would never rival those of Longfellow or Tennyson, nor be quoted extensively. In fact, he concealed his poetry in the body of his letter so that it dawned only slowly on the casual reader that, at irregular intervals, the words began to rhyme. These are some of his verses:

Experience in Indian fighting on the plain,
Gave me some slight knowledge how to guard a wagon train.
My Sergeant William Raycraft really was the fellow,
Who should have had the Medal, and that of Metal yellow.
Certainly patient "bushwhacking" was all we had to do,
And smile at thought of how wildly rebel bullets flew.
If you would have me more enlarge,
I will hereafter describe said charge.
Success attend you and your book,
I am glad the work you undertook.

In a personal sketch of the service for which his medal was awarded, First Lieutenant Charles L. Barrell of the 1st Michigan Colored Regiment (later redesignated as the 102nd Regiment, U.S. Colored Troops) described an action that certainly can be said to have taken place behind enemy lines. Yet the situation at that time

" '. . . Indian fighting on the plain,/Gave me some slight knowledge how to guard a wagon train.' "—Wood engraving, Frank Leslie's Illustrated Newspaper, *from a sketch by Edwin Forbes of an attack by some of Mosby's men upon a wagon train* (LIBRARY OF CONGRESS)

in South Carolina in the middle of April 1865, over a week after the surrender at Appomattox, was such that the words "front lines" scarcely apply.

"I enlisted in Company D, 17th Michigan Infantry, under Captain Julius C. Burrows, August 2, 1862. My history from the time of my enlistment to November 16, 1863, is the same as thousands of others who were with me during those trying times from 1861 to 1865. On November 16, 1863, I received an order from the War Department to report to Colonel H. Barnes at Detroit, which closed my service with the 17th Michigan Infantry.

"We were then situated in Tennessee, with no railroad connection for many weary miles over the mountains. I packed my knapsack, bid goodbye to my comrades, and started on a lonely march. This was a very dangerous undertaking, considering that bushwhackers and guerrillas infested the mountains to pick off lone and unprotected travelers, and especially Union soldiers. I walked to Nicholasville, Kentucky, and there got transportation to Detroit, and reported to Colonel Barnes, November 29, 1863. I was assigned as a second lieutenant in Company C, 1st Michigan Colored Regiment, then being raised in Detroit. . . .

"We left Detroit March 28, 1864, for Annapolis, Maryland, and remained at that place until the 15th of April. Then we embarked on transports to Hilton Head, South Carolina. Colonel Barnes resigned and Captain Henry L. Chipman was appointed colonel of the regiment. We were employed on picket duty for a month and then sent to Beaufort, South Carolina, thence to Baldwin, Florida where we destroyed the railroad . . . and then returned to Beaufort.

"We left Beaufort to join General Foster's command at Boyd's Landing. We were engaged with the enemy at Honey Hill, and took part in other minor engagements until the 9th of March, 1865, when we were ordered to garrison the city of Savannah, where we remained until the 28th. Then we were ordered to Charleston, South Carolina. We arrived there the 1st of April, 1865, and, on the 11th, the right wing, under the command of Colonel Chipman, marched under orders to join General Potter on the Santee River. We struck it at Nelson's Ferry about seventy miles from Charleston. General Potter had arrived and pushed on; Colonel Chipman determined to follow General Potter, whom he had ascertained had gone in the direction of Camden, South Carolina. The enemy kept increasing in numbers and it steadily became apparent that we were being surrounded and drawn into a net which would ultimately result in capture or death.

"Colonel Chipman, determined to try and communicate with General Potter, sent for me and asked if I would undertake to get through the rebel lines and inform General Potter of our situation. I gladly gave my consent, although I had marched all day and was officer of the picket the night before, getting no sleep. At dark I bade goodbye to my brother officers, not expecting ever to see them again, for it was a good twenty-five miles to General Potter's command through a strange country infested by the enemy's troops. The roads were full of debris such as broken wagons, and I proceeded very cautiously at first, and many times dismounted and crawled up to burning wagons which I thought to be rebel picket posts. I finally pushed boldly ahead, galloping at times, but using caution, especially in the woods.

"I came to a point where the road forked and I was puzzled for some time to know which angle General Potter's command had taken. I dismounted and looked for the wide tracks made by the wheels of the cannon carriages for more than a half mile up both forks. I failed to find any trace of them but finally, to my joy, I found a track which proved to be the right road. Many little incidents took place to keep the nerves of myself and my orderly strung to the highest point.

"We were galloping full speed when my orderly's horse stumbled, turning completely over. Drawing rein, I found the horse with its head doubled under, and the man, or rather boy as he was, under the horse. I asked if he was hurt, to which he replied that he would not know until he was released. After I had got the horse up, my plucky companion got up and brushed off his clothes. We pushed on until we came to a house from the window of which shown a light. We called 'Halloo' and a man's voice responded without opening the door. I asked him if any Yankees had passed by there during the day. Upon an affirmative response, I asked how many and received the reply, 'A right smart of them.' Although the information I received was of no material benefit, it informed me that I was on the right road.

"We left the house as fast as possible but had not been long on the way when I heard in our front the snort or cough of a horse.

I did not know whether it was friend or foe, but felt almost certain that it must be the latter. We were soon challenged: 'Who goes there?,' to which I replied: 'A friend.'

"I received the order to advance and give the countersign. I knew then that he was a rebel. We charged forward and captured an orderly to Colonel Smith of the 26th South Carolina Regiment. . . . I learned from him that General Potter was in Camden; that the enemy was posted on all roads leading into that place. We would be obliged to abandon our horses and take to the woods and swamps. But to fail to get through meant destruction to Colonel Chipman and his little band, for no quarter was given colored sol-

" '. . . to fail to get through meant destruction to Colonel Chipman and his little band . . .' "
—Charles L. Barrell soon after the Civil War
(KOHEN COLLECTION)

diers or their officers by the enemy. This was well understood by all of the colored people and their officers during the rebellion.

"I told the rebel orderly that if he did not guide me safely through to General Potter's camp that night or undertook, in any way, to mislead me, I would shoot him on the spot. I placed my own orderly in front of the rebel, with myself in the rear, holding my pistol at the back of the rebel's head. In this way we marched through impassable woods and swamps, reaching the camp of General Potter just about daylight.

"Turning my prisoner over to the Provost Marshal, I lost no

time in communicating with General Potter. Upon hearing of the situation, he gave me a battalion of the 4th Massachusetts Cavalry, commanded by Major Webster, and furnished me with another horse. After breakfast we immediately started back to the assistance of Colonel Chipman. We found the enemy posted behind breastworks and slowly closing about Colonel Chipman and his little band. We immediately charged them in their rear, taking them completely by surprise. Not knowing how large our force was, they fled, scattering in every direction. The forces of Major Webster and Colonel Chipman joined and a general handshaking took place. We immediately began a backward march to join General Potter, which was accomplished at sunset. I was so nearly exhausted that, although a heavy rainstorm had taken place, I fell asleep in a few moments without supper."

From beginning to end it took eight long months for the northern armies and fleets to capture the southern fortress of Vicksburg. The first unsuccessful attempt was made in November and December 1862; the final venture began late in March 1863; the surrender of the city did not take place until July 4, 1863. The story of this campaign provides more fascinating reading of an unusual nature than any other in the war. The leaders, the officers, and the men on both sides exhibited extraordinary ingenuity and resourcefulness in this unique contest, fought on dry land, in bayous and swamps, and on the broad waters of "The Father of Waters," the Mississippi River.

The adventurous experiment for which Captain William H. Ward volunteered, and for which he received the Army's Congressional Medal of Honor thirty-one and a half years later, took place on the night of May 3, 1863. On this date, General Ulysses S. Grant, with two corps, was at Grand Gulf, Mississippi, several miles south of Vicksburg. General William Tecumseh Sherman, commanding the Fifteenth Corps, was still north of Vicksburg at Milliken's Bend. Sherman was worried that Grant might run short of supplies. He had no way of knowing that Grant had made the momentous decision to cut loose from his base, abandon his line of communications and advance into enemy territory, taking with him only what could be carried, making the country furnish the balance of his needs.

In April, most of the fleet had managed to run past the Vicks-

burg batteries with not too great a loss of ships or men. In order
to send supplies to Grant's army by the fastest route, it was decided
to send some barges to run the gauntlet, but the conditions as described by Captain Ward were by no means favorable.

Before telling the story of what happened to him and his men,
there was one point which Captain Ward was anxious to clarify.
He commanded Company B of the 47th Ohio Infantry but, as he
carefully explained, he himself came from Adrian, Michigan, and
all his men were from his home state.

"I recruited this company at my own expense, expecting to be
assigned to a Michigan regiment. Failing in this because of the
state's quota being full, and being offered a position in a regiment
then being organized at Cincinnati, Ohio if I would take my company to that city, the proposition was accepted; and thus the company became a part of the 47th Ohio Volunteer Infantry, though
composed wholly of Michigan men.

"While the 15th Army Corps was camped at Milliken's Bend on
May 3, 1863, General W. T. Sherman, commanding the left wing of
the army before Vicksburg, decided to try the experiment of sending supplies to General Grant then at Grand Gulf some fifty miles
below, by floating them down the Mississippi River past the Vicksburg batteries, taking chances on the fiery ordeal the boats were
sure to receive in transit. Heretofore, under the most favorable circumstances of the darkest nights, and a convoy of ironclads to draw
the fire of the enemy's guns while the other boats ran by at full
speed, about three-fourths of the boats attempting this hazardous
enterprise had escaped destruction.

"On this occasion, however, conditions were changed to an extent as to almost invite destruction and capture. The one little expedition must not only receive the concentrated fire of every gun
the enemy could bring to bear on the river, but not a cloud ob-
structed the rays of a full moon that made the night one of the
lightest of the year. The expedition as fitted out consisted of two
large unwieldy barges, loaded with forage and provisions, propelled
by a small towboat securely lashed between. If the expedition survived the storm of shot and shell from the miles of batteries which
lined the shore of the river in and around Vicksburg, the supplies
would reach Grant's army in about eight hours, a work that would
require as many days to accomplish if sent overland.

"'Heretofore, under the most favorable circumstances of the darkest nights, and a convoy of ironclads to draw the fire of the enemy's guns while the other boats ran by at full speed, about three-fourths of the boats attempting this hazardous enterprise had escaped destruction.'"—Photo of a painting belonging to Admiral Porter, depicting the first part of his fleet running past the Vicksburg batteries on the night of April 16, 1863
(LIBRARY OF CONGRESS)

"The extremely hazardous character of the undertaking, rendered doubly so for reasons stated, precluded the detailing of men to man the expedition, and volunteers were called for. Notwithstanding the desperate chances of success, yielding to the doctrine of possibilities, and without a moment's thought as to probable consequences, I promptly volunteered for the work and was directed by Brigadier General Hugh Ewing to select volunteers from my own company sufficient to protect the expedition from possible capture by boarders, and a sufficient number of rivermen to man and operate the tug. This after some delay being accomplished, at 9 o'clock we repaired on board and I found myself in command of as strange and queer looking a craft as ever navigated water. The little towboat was completely hidden between and seemingly protected by the heavily loaded barges on either side, and looked a pigmy beside the barges she was expected to propel to destination. When we were about ready to start Messrs. A. D. Richardson, Junius Henri Browne, and A. D. Colburn, army correspondents for New York papers, introduced themselves and asked permission to accompany the expedition as passengers, stating that they were enroute to Grant's headquarters and desired to avail themselves of this means of reaching their destination. While regretting our lack of passenger accommodations, permission was reluctantly granted, and at ten o'clock the lines were cast off and our craft was soon steaming down the river.

"Up to this time I had supposed that all needful precautions for safety had been taken but now learned upon examination that they were altogether inadequate. Indeed the expedition was so carelessly organized as to almost invite destruction. We had only two buckets and not a single skiff. Two tugs were requisite to steer the unwieldy craft and enable us to run twelve miles per hour; with one we could only accomplish seven miles, aided by a strong Mississippi current.

"There were thirty-five persons on board, all volunteers, consisting of fourteen men of Company B, 47th Ohio Volunteers, the tug's

" 'Indeed the expedition was so carelessly organized as to almost invite destruction.' "—Captain William H. Ward
(KOHEN COLLECTION)

crew and other officers, soldiers, and citizens enroute to Grant's army. For three hours we glided silently along the glassy waters between banks festooned with heavy drooping foliage, presenting in the bright moonlight a scene of surpassing grandeur.

"At one o'clock in the morning a rocket shot up from the Mississippi shore and exploded high in the air, signaling the enemy of our approach. Ten minutes later we saw the flash and heard the boom of their first gun. Much practice on similar occasions had given them excellent range. The shell struck one of the barges and exploded upon it, and we were soon under heavy fire. The range of the batteries covered the river for nearly seven miles. The Mississippi here is very crooked, resembling the letter S, and at some points we passed within two hundred yards of ten-inch guns, with point-blank range upon us.

"As we moved around the bends the shots came toward us at once from the right, left, front, and rear. Inclination born of curiosity to look into the craters of these volcanoes, as they poured forth sheets of flame and volleys of shot and shell, had joined with a sort of daredevil fearlessness in impelling me to volunteer for this expedition. I wanted to learn how one would feel as he slowly glided past them and ascertained to my fullest satisfaction as I stood on the deck of the tug directing the man at the wheel how and where to steer.

"Discretion prompted me to cower close to the wheelhouse for partial shelter from the storm of shot and shell that came from all directions. Great sheets of flame leaped up and spread out from the enemy's guns as shot and shells came screaming and shrieking through the air, rattled and crashed as they penetrated the sides of the barges, or exploded on board in great fountains of fire. It was a scene little calculated to awaken sentimental memories, yet as I look back at that picture through the vista of more than thirty years Tennyson's lines ring in my ears:

> Cannon to right of them
> Cannon to left of them
> Cannon in front of them
> Volleyed and thundered
> Stormed at by shot and shell
> Boldly they rode and well

Into the jaws of death
Into the mouth of hell
Rode the six hundred.

"A large shell exploded on board the little tug near the engine room, tearing away a portion of the smokestack and covering the boat with flying splinters and debris. I listened, for the moment, for the reassuring puff, puff, puff of the little engine, and hearing it, said to myself, 'Thus far, at least, we are all right.' We were now below the town, having run five miles of batteries. Ten minutes more meant safety. And I already began to congratulate myself upon our success and good fortune, when the scene suddenly changed. A crash, and a terrific report like the explosion of a magazine, made the tug and barges rock and reel like an earthquake, and the air was filled with volumes of escaping steam, smoke, cinders, burning coals, missiles, and fragments of every description. It was accompanied by a shriek which I shall never forget, though it occupied but a second of time. It was the death cry of the pilot as he stood at the wheel. A blow, and with a reeling sensation of dizziness and weariness, I sank to the deck of the tug, insensible.

"How long I remained in that condition cannot be told. I have a dim recollection of returning consciousness, hearing sounds of guns and explosions of shells, but they seemed a long way off, and later of voices, and of hearing my name spoken, but so far away as to be hardly distinguishable. Later I realized that I was in the water, and shortly after, of being raised to a sitting posture, and a friendly voice inquired if I was badly hurt.

"I was lifted to my feet and seemed to stand on something solid, but in the water, and soon realized that the tug had sunk as far as the lines which lashed her to the barges she was towing would permit, bringing her deck a few inches below the surface of the water. I was soon lifted to the top of the hay bales on one of the barges and had a confused idea that something serious had happened.

"I again listened for the friendly voice of the tug, but it was silent while the place where it had once been was filled with broken timbers and wreckage floating upon the surface of the water, and from the shore there came scattering, shrill, sharp, ragged rebel yells so familiar to every man who has been at the front. I had heard that yell many times but never when it appeared so exultant as now, while the enemy's batteries seemed to ply their guns with redoubled vigor. A shot passed so near my face that I felt the wind, and seeing fire near me directed one of the men to extinguish it. Notwithstanding the storm of shot and shell and even musketry which rained about us, the man actually laughed as he pointed to the blaze, and I realized the uselessness of the effort as I looked upon the volumes of flames that rose high in the air, and saw that the barges were on fire from stem to stern, except a small place at the bow of each where the crews had congregated. It was only a question of a very few minutes when all hands would be driven into the river. The shell that struck the tug had done fearful execution. It had killed the pilot, engineer, and fireman, exploded the boiler, then passed to the furnace where it exploded, tearing the tug asunder, throwing up great sheets of glowing coals upon both barges, from which the bales of dry hay caught like tinder, and we were now a wreck floating helplessly before the enemy's guns which were still playing upon us.

"Realizing that the first thing to do, if possible, was to stop their firing, I gave a soldier my handkerchief with instructions to wave it as a signal of surrender, which upon being recognized by the enemy the firing soon ceased. Looking in the direction of the other barge I beheld Mr. Richardson in the act of floating off on a bale of hay. When a shot struck it, he disappeared beneath the water amid a sheet of foam. For a moment I supposed him killed, but in a few seconds he came to the surface and called to his associates to throw overboard another hay bale upon which he floated off, and I was agreeably surprised at its seeming buoyancy.

"It does not often happen to men in one-quarter of an hour to see death in as many forms as confronted those on board that ill-fated expedition: by shot and shell, scalding, burning, and drowning. It was uncomfortable but less exciting than one might suppose. The memory of it through all the years that have elapsed since then is far more impressive than the experience.

" 'Can't we surrender?,' called a poor scalded fellow to one of the newspaper men. 'The devil you say,' replied the Bohemian, 'I think we will fight them.' The remark was doubtless creditable to the gentleman's pugnacity, but just then our fighting qualities were, in ring parlance, 'knocked out.' The fire now made it necessary that everybody take to the water upon anything that would float. The

wounded and scalded were first to receive attention by being carefully placed upon bales of hay with an able-bodied man in like
manner floating alongside to care for his unfortunate comrade, and
if possible guide the novel rafts to the Louisiana shore. After which
all hands floated off in like manner, and I recollect mentally spec-
ulating as to how long my novel craft would probably float before
becoming waterlogged and useless, and regretting that circumstances prevented my securing two bales instead of one. Our troops
occupied the Louisiana shore some ten miles below, the intervening
distance being covered by rebel batteries and pickets. If unmolested
we could reach our friends about daylight by floating, otherwise
surrender was the only alternative.

"The enemy by this time had ceased firing and shouted, 'Have
you no boats?' Learning that we had none, they sent out a yawl.
As it approached me, I requested them to rescue the wounded first,
with which they at once complied. Another yawl soon made its appearance. In the bow was seated a Confederate soldier who raised
his musket and ordered me to surrender. Bruised and scalded as I
was, I was struck with the ludicrousness of the demand but hastened
to assure him that my intentions were peaceable. I was ordered
into the boat where I found one of the newspaper men and three
badly scalded men of the tug's crew whose agony was heartrending.

"We were soon taken ashore where we found the other survivors
and there in the moonlight, surrounded by rebel bayonets, the roll
was called, to which just sixteen, less than half our original number, responded alive. Some of the scalded men were piteous spec-
tacles. The raw flesh appeared almost ready to drop from their faces
and hands, as they ran about half wild with excruciating pain. The
injuries of the wounded were less serious, being mostly severe con-
tusions, though two had arms broken, and one a dislocated ankle.
The missing numbered ten, not one of whom was ever heard from
afterward.

"With difficulty we were marched to the city, our captors assisting in transporting the wounded. After being registered by the Provost Marshal, the injured were sent to a hospital, and the balance
escorted to the city jail, where we learned during the forenoon that
our scalded comrades had died of their injuries at one of the military
hospitals in the city.

"During the day our party was taken before General Bowen,

commander of the post, who received us courteously and asked many questions concerning the location and strength of our forces, General Grant's probable intentions, etc. Finding us wary in our answers, however, he soon changed the subject to the incidents of our adventures of the night before, and expressed much surprise that men should attempt to run a boat past their batteries, especially on so light a night. Upon hearing our complaints of the accommodations provided at the jail, the general directed that our party be quartered in the second story of the county courthouse, until sent elsewhere.

"Arriving at the courthouse we were met by Major Watts, the Confederate Commissioner for Exchange of Prisoners, by whom the members of our party were paroled, but informed at the same time that it was necessary to send us to Richmond as the cartel for exchange of prisoners at Vicksburg had been suspended. The Major, however, attempted to rally our somewhat dampened if not depressed spirits with the jocose remark: 'Gentlemen, you are in a strange land, and in the hands of strangers, but keep a stiff upper lip, and don't be discouraged. We expect to have General Grant in this same predicament in a few days.' To which we replied that Grant would be in Vicksburg sure enough, but not in the capacity of a prisoner of war. Later on, when Vicksburg surrendered, the writer, who had been exchanged and rejoined the army the night before, meeting Major Watts in the same room at the courthouse, good-naturedly recalled the incident by saying: 'Major, Grant is in Vicksburg as we both predicted and *our* positions are reversed. Don't be discouraged, however, when I tell you an open secret, we are going to have Jeff Davis in this same fix in a few weeks.'

"On the morning of May 6th our party, consisting of the three correspondents, two officers, and about fifty other prisoners were taken to the depot and started for Richmond, guarded by a detachment of soldiers from the 27th Louisiana Confederate Infantry, commanded by a Captain Robertson, who treated his prisoners with every consideration consistent with the rules of war, and with whom we were soon on friendly terms. To recount the scenes and incidents of that journey would fill a volume. Our treatment by the people along the route was at times pleasant and social, and at others morose to a studied severity. At Demopolis, Alabama, a number of ladies came to the depot attended by a retinue of servants carrying baskets filled with lunches of bread and fried chicken which they distributed among the prisoners, refusing compensation therefor, with the remark that if we ever met any Southern soldiers in like adverse circumstances and would return the favor, they would be amply rewarded. At Montgomery, we stopped over Sunday and some of our party attended church escorted by a Confederate soldier, where we subsequently learned the presence of a blue uniform attracted quite as much attention as the discourse of the officiating minister.

"At Selma, our Louisiana guards took leave of us and were succeeded by a detail from the 31st Alabama, commanded by a lieutenant whose name I have forgotten, who escorted our party to Atlanta, Georgia. These men like the Louisianians had seen service and smelled powder and treated their prisoners with every respect consistent with their duties as soldiers, and with whom we were soon on friendly terms. But on arriving at Atlanta there was a change in the program. We were placed in the charge of some Georgia home guards by whom every privilege or favor was studiously and ofttimes insultingly ignored. Our newspaper friends, chagrined at this new turn of affairs, sought to relieve the restraint by invoking the influence of the press of Atlanta in their behalf, by sending out their cards to the several newspapers of the city requesting an exchange of courtesies usual among members of the craft. The only response was an editorial in one of the morning dailies the following day, calling attention to the fact and refusing all intercourse with Northern journalists, and particularly with attachés of 'Old Greeley's *New York Tribune*,' who were justly entitled to receive the most rigorous treatment at the hands of an outraged Southern people. That morning our squad of prisoners, now numbering about sixty officers, soldiers, and civilians, was taken to the Atlanta depot, closely guarded by a detachment of Georgia home guards, and resumed our journey toward Richmond where we confidently expected to be exchanged. But these fond anticipations were soon blasted on our arrival in that city where, on being taken to the famous bastile, Libby Prison, we were informed that the paroles given us at Vicksburg were valueless because of an interruption in the cartel, and that the exchange of prisoners was for the time being suspended. We were conducted to the office of the Commandant, Major Turner, where, after being registered,

searched, and relieved of our valuables, and receipts given therefor, we were escorted into a darkened room filled with other war
prisoners. They received us with many shouts of, 'More Yanks,
More Yanks, Fresh fish,' etc. but at once crowded around, plying
us with questions for news of the progress of the war and the condition of the affairs of the North. Many of these men had been prisoners for months and the only news obtainable was from Southern
newspapers which were always highly colored in favor of the Confederacy. Their anxiety to learn the true condition of affairs was
easily understood.

"As my eyes became accustomed to the darkness my attention
was attracted to a legend which some wag had written with char-
coal upon the whitewashed wall, 'Who enters here leaves hope behind.' The effect upon the mind of one who for the first time finds
himself restrained of liberty in a place of such unenviable reputation was peculiar. Later, however, I learned to appreciate and enter
into any kind of a practical joke at the expense of newly arrived
prisoners. Our party consisting of the three correspondents, the
writer, and one other officer was soon transferred to a room in the
third story where we lost our individuality and were simply known
as Mess No. 21.

"It is proper to add in this connection that, being exchanged
some weeks later, on leaving the prison I presented my receipt at
the office of the Commandant and received back all the money and
valuables taken from me on entering the prison, a practice I am
informed was subsequently not in vogue."

XIV

A Bugle Pealed

HISTORY teaches us that civil wars, wars of rebellion, up-heavals within a country, are the most brutal, the most savagely fought of all wars, with no quarter asked or given on either side. When section is divided against section, family against family, hatreds are more deeply felt and more harshly expressed. Violence without restraint soon becomes the way of life. The results are vicious murders, shootings, and hangings. Gangs of ruthless killers appear, operating between the lines, hanging upon the fringes of the armies, preying upon the helpless of both sides. Whispered accusations based on nothing but suspicion, resentment, or greed will be followed by sudden burning, looting, destruction, and the murder of entirely innocent people. This is the record of history and when the wars are eventually won or lost, the defeated are relentlessly pursued, persecuted, and the leaders executed without the slightest hope of mercy or forgiveness.

Yet, with very few exceptions, in the American Civil War or the War Between the States the exact opposite was true. Fraternization between the lines during the periods of inactivity was common. The men of both armies often got together to trade items in short supply, tell tall tales, and swap lies. Some officers feared that this would result in less zealous action when battle was again resumed but it did nothing of the sort. During the winter of 1862–63 in the lines facing each other across the Rappahannock near Fredericksburg, army bands serenaded friend and foe alike, taking turns playing each other's favorite songs. Yet the record shows that the Battles of Chancellorsville and Gettysburg that followed in May and July were waged with the highest degree of courage, bravery, and zealous devotion to the causes for which the soldiers fought.

Never in any war have the combatants shown a greater respect and admiration for their enemies. Courageous acts were applauded by both sides even while they were shooting at each other. A help-less man lying between the lines would become an object of mercy, and might be aided by men from either side. Soldiers would risk their own lives to save that of a wounded enemy.

Evacuation of the wounded under combat conditions is always a problem. In a daylight withdrawal, or retreat under fire, it be-comes extremely difficult, if not impossible. Forrester L. Taylor, who had been an accountant in Burlington, New Jersey, when the war broke out, described his efforts at Chancellorsville.

"At the Battle of Chancellorsville, Virginia, May 3, 1863, our regiment, the 23rd New Jersey Volunteer Infantry, 1st Brigade, 1st Division, Sixth Corps, Army of the Potomac, occupied the extreme left of the field. We were exposed to a very severe fire; the line was frequently broken and the regiment repulsed. During one of the many ineffectual charges made, my 2nd Lieutenant, Richard J. Wilson, went down with three wounds.

"Later in the afternoon, through a perfect hail of lead and iron from the Southern forces, our line scattered in all directions. I started off at a run, but had gone but a few yards when I felt a hand laid upon my shoulder. I considered myself a prisoner but was rejoiced to hear the familiar tones of my friend, 1st Lieutenant Charles Sibley of Company A, who said: 'Hold up, Taylor. It is bad enough for us to have to turn our backs on those fellows, without running away.' Passing his arm through mine, he walked toward the rear with the same placid indifference as a flaneur on Broad-way. After going some few hundred yards amid a hail of bullets, we noticed our colonel, E. Burd Grubb, Brevet Brigadier General, rallying a handful of men on our left. Sibley said, 'I am going in here.' At this moment I was called by Lieutenant Wilson, lying near, who said: 'For God's sake, Taylor, carry me off the field. I have been in a Rebel prison once as a well man. If I go back as I am, it will kill me.'

"I glanced toward the colonel and recognized that with his mere handful he could accomplish nothing against the rapidly advanc-ing Confederate force. So, bidding Sibley good-bye, I remained by the side of Wilson. I could not carry him alone, but shortly, one by one, three men of the company came up and, with perfect cool-ness, obeyed my request to carry off Wilson. We placed him on a blanket, each one of us taking one corner. We had not proceeded

" 'We placed him on a blanket, each one of us taking one corner.' "—Pencil
and Chinese white drawing by Alfred R. Waud, showing wounded soldiers
being carried from the Wilderness battlefield

very far when, seeing our men again breaking, I glanced behind
and found the Confederates not over thirty yards back. Hastily ex-
plaining to Wilson that I could not consent to have four men captured, and yet do him no service, I took his watch and purse and
all of us made for the rear. In the meantime, the Union line was
formed in front of us and we were exposed to the fire of both armies.
This stand was successful; the enemy was repulsed and, before we
reached this new formed line, they were in full retreat.

"I therefore took my three brave boys and returned to Wilson.
We gathered him up again. The Confederate line was reformed.
When we had nearly reached our lines we were arrested by a loud
cry. Directly in front of us was a Union battery, whose commander,
seeing our humane occupation, was loath to fire on us. Yet the

Confederates were so close in our rear that delay was dangerous. We were right by the side of a deep gully. With one impulse we jumped in, wounded man and all, as a shower of grape from double-shotted guns passed over our heads. The Confederates were unable to stand such a severe fire at close quarters. We were soon enabled to get the poor fellow from the gully and shortly afterwards had him in the hands of the surgeon, for which we then, nor afterwards, ever received one word of thanks.

"Returning Wilson his purse and watch, we went at once to the front. Company and regimental formations were, by this time, lost. Men of all regiments were fighting side by side without regard thereto. Here we remained until the day's action was over.

"While carrying off Wilson, I had been called by Corporal Joel W. Wainwright of my Company, a boy who had exhibited courage so brilliant in the opening of the engagement as to capture my entire heart. He had gone down with a bullet in his ankle, and requested me to get him to safety as well. I replied: 'I can do nothing for you now, Corporal, but may later.'

"After getting Wilson in, I did not feel justified in remaining longer from the line of battle. Under other circumstances I would not have asked my men, tired as they were after doing picket duty all night and fighting all day, to return to the field. But Wainwright's gallantry demanded recognition. I explained to my three boys that he was too brave to be permitted to fall in the hands of the Rebels. They cheerfully acquiesced. After a short rest and a little food, we started forth.

"The Confederates had possession of the field and fired on us as soon as we showed ourselves beyond our lines. We proceeded, however, and on reaching Wainwright placed him on a blanket, and returned to our lines without accident and, as may be imagined, without unnecessary delay, placing him in the hands of the surgeons. Differing from Wilson, thirty-four years has not been sufficient time to permit the full expression of his gratitude.

"I then learned that Lieutenant Charles Sibley had fallen shortly after leaving me on the field. I remembered the spot well from a peculiar landmark, and again asked my boys to return with me for him. They never failed me. But on this trip we were stopped by our pickets refusing to permit us to pass. Requesting my men to await my return, I sought Colonel Grubb for the necessary permit.

He told me he was powerless but was willing to accompany me to the brigade commander, Colonel W. H. Penrose of the 15th New Jersey Volunteers. They both endeavored to dissuade me but, on hearing of our long friendship, and Sibley's gallantry, Colonel Penrose said: 'Captain, I don't care to have four men killed in an endeavor to rescue an officer who in all probability is now dead.' He, however, granted me a pass conditional on my immediate return if the danger was great. Before we could reach the spot where Sibley lay the fire became so severe that, agreeable to promise, I returned reluctantly to camp.

"The body of poor Sibley was buried within the Southern lines; H Company of an Alabama regiment sending over his cap and shoulder straps, with a letter stating that he had been given a soldier's burial. This was by flag of truce, after we crossed the Rappahannock River, on May 5, 1863.

"Although we had been exposed to heavy fire, sometimes from both armies, not one of us was wounded. Twice we were, with Wilson, almost within Southern reach; but whether they forbore from magnanimity, or from an expectation of our capture, who can say?

"My three brave boys, who stood so gallantly by me, I promoted on the field to be non-commissioned officers. As more is expected from an officer, they were more entitled to a Medal of Honor than myself and, after I was so decorated, I would have recommended them. But they have long since entered into their eternal sleep. If mine does, their names *also* deserve mention. They are:

> Sergeant Thomas McBreen promoted from Corporal,
> Corporal Richmond Ayers appointed from Private,
> Corporal Elijah Earling appointed from Private,

May 3, 1863, to date from May 1, 1863, for gallantry at Chancellorsville, Virginia.

"I regarded this as an ordinary occurrence yet, for it, I, thirty-three years afterwards, received the highest honor the government can bestow.

> "*Forrester L. Taylor*
> "Captain, H Co., 23d & 34th N.J. Vols.
> "Brevet Major, U.S. Vols."

Judging from what happened on the same day on another part of the battlefield, there can be little doubt that the southern soldiers (who knew a brave man when they saw one), "forbore from magnanimity."

When asked to tell how he had won his Medal of Honor, Thomas W. Bradley of Walden, Orange County, New York, responded by sending news clippings describing the event. The newspaper account contained affidavits that had been prepared by former soldiers and submitted to the Secretary of War asking that Bradley's heroism be recognized.

One of the affidavits was written by a Thomas Hart. It described the situation immediately preceding the event:

"I was present and on duty at the Battle of Chancellorsville, and was at that time a corporal of Company A. During the battle on May 3, 1863 . . . our regiment lost severely in killed and wounded, but held the line until our ammunition was almost exhausted, when we were withdrawn to the plain near Chancellorsville House. The Confederates having driven our battery from its position, we were ordered to recapture it at the point of the bayonet and did so, but were compelled to vacate and, under a heavy fire of grape and canister, fell rapidly back east of the Chancellorsville House, where our division . . . had been forced to a new line. While in this position our colonel, A. Van Horne Ellis, suggested making a detail to bring in ammunition from boxes strapped to the backs of dead mules lying between the lines."

No one wanted to order any man to go out between the lines, across the open plain, swept by fire, to cut the ammunition boxes off the mules and bring them back. Yet the regiment, the 124th New York Infantry, nicknamed the "Orange Blossoms," had expended almost all the ammunition it had on hand. The only alternative was to make another retreat which could open a big hole in the Union lines. Young Bradley of Company H, only nineteen years old, suggested that a call be made for volunteers. But when the men were asked to go, he was the only one to respond.

Alone, Bradley started running forward. He reached one of the mules and, lying down behind it, cut the strap holding the ammunition boxes and started back across the field. By this time the Confederates had realized the importance of his mission. He became the target for their fire; it seemed impossible that he could

survive. Suddenly, according to the eyewitness accounts, Bradley turned and began walking backward. He explained later that he felt sure he would be hit, and preferred it be in the front rather than from behind. This action undoubtedly saved his life, for the Confederates were quick to sense the significance of his action. Every gun along the line stopped firing. The southerners not only held their fire but waved their caps and cheered him until he reached the Union lines.

In later years Thomas Bradley became a prominent figure in Orange County, which includes Newburgh, Goshen, and West Point, New York, and was four times elected to Congress to represent the 20th (now the 27th) District.

Now let us turn back the calendar one day to another part of the same battlefield of Chancellorsville. There another call was being made for volunteers. This time four men responded: Private William W. Cranston, Sergeant Henry Heller, Private Elisha B. Seaman, and Sergeant Thomas Thompson, all of Company A, 66th Ohio Infantry.

The mission was an act of mercy; it was to go out between the lines while the battle was being fought and bring in a wounded Confederate officer. In Henry Heller's words: "On the second day's fight at Chancellorsville, Virginia, General Joseph Hooker called for four men of my company to volunteer to enter the enemy's lines under two heavy fires, Union and Rebel, and bring in a Rebel who was in great distress, having his leg shot off from our battery. For this act I was awarded the medal."

Former sergeant Heller of Urbana, Ohio, seemed keenly interested in having the remainder of his wartime service recorded. First, he had served three months as one of the 75,000 volunteers called for in President Lincoln's proclamation issued right after the fall of Fort Sumter. Then he had reenlisted and served an additional three years and three months. He named fourteen battles in which he had been engaged, including such famous names as Second Bull Run, Antietam, Gettysburg, Missionary Ridge, and Atlanta, "was wounded once, and marched eleven thousand miles. This is the 66th O.V.I. Record of the War."

On the form provided, Henry Heller noted that he had entered his last battle "voluntarily, my time having expired a short time before, and I was relieved from duty."

His life after the conclusion of the war had not been as rewarding as that of Bradley, for he was the soldier quoted in an earlier chapter as having written: "Please write when your book is completed and give me a price list. If able, will buy one. Am poor and broken down, but will try for a book."

Here, at Chancellorsville, a wounded Confederate officer had been brought off the field by four Union soldiers. Exactly two months later, in the fury of the Battle of Gettysburg, a Union officer's life was saved, under fire, by a Confederate.

The Union officer was himself engaged in trying to help a wounded soldier.

"The story in full of 'How I won the Medal' is rather long, but I will condense it for the purposes of your book. It was at the Battle of Gettysburg. I was a 1st Lieutenant, Company A, 140th Pennsylvania Volunteer Infantry, 3rd Brigade (Zook's), 1st Division (Caldwell's), Second Corps (Hancock's).

"On the afternoon of July 2, 1863, my brigade had charged across the historic 'Wheatfield' and driven the enemy into the woods beyond. In turn we were driven back, our ranks broken up in the woods and among the rocks. When we emerged from the woods

"Never in any war have the combatants shown a greater respect and

and were about to retreat across the Wheatfield, the only man of my company whom I could see was Orderly Sergeant J. M. Piper. At this moment we came across a comrade whom I did not know, wounded badly in the legs. He cried out, 'Comrades, carry me off!'

admiration for their enemies."—Painting by Franklin D. Briscoe of the "Whirlpool in the Wheatfield"

I replied that we could not do that as the enemy was too close upon us, but immediately noticed two rocks nearby suitable for protection from the enemy's fire, and said to the orderly sergeant, 'Come help me and we will put him between these rocks.'

"With the assistance of the sergeant, I carried him and placed him between these rocks in an apparent place of safety. I remained with him long enough to straighten out his limbs and take his hand and say 'goodbye.' But this delay of a few minutes caused the enemy to gain upon me so much that it proved fatal to my intention of crossing the Wheatfield and reaching our reserves on the opposite side. Within a few yards of me the enemy called out, 'Halt, you damned Yankee, Halt!'

"I did not obey this command and, in consequence, a few moments later received a gunshot in my left leg below the knee, crushing both bones, and fell instantly to the ground, the enemy charging over me.

"Unable to crawl off, I lay on the field all night and the next day, between the fires of both armies. About the middle of the afternoon of July 3, '63, I received a second gunshot wound passing through my right leg. Some time after this I was carried within the Confederate lines by Lieutenant Thomas P. Oliver, adjutant 24th Georgia, C.S.A., and was given a canteen of water, and placed in the edge of the woods under the shade of the trees.

"In performing this act of mercy, the Confederate officer was truly heroic, being all the time, while carrying me off, more or less exposed to the fires of both armies.

"As a result of my wounds, my left leg was amputated on the morning of July 4, '63, and the strength and motion of my right leg was impaired. Since the war I have ascertained that the unknown comrade whose life I tried to save was John Buckley, Company B of my own regiment, and that he died from loss of blood and exposure before help could reach him.

"*J. J. Purman, M.D.*
"#1435 Chapin Street, N.W.
"Washington, D.C."

When the day came, nearly two years later, for the formal surrender at Appomattox, it was Joshua L. Chamberlain, the leader of the counterattack of the 20th Maine on Little Round Top at Gettysburg, who was selected to command the Union troops. The day was April 12, 1865, three days after the historic meeting of General Grant and General Lee.

General Chamberlain stood with the color guard at the head of two brigades of Union infantry, waiting for the Confederate army to march from its bivouac and lay down its arms and flags. Here they came with the old swinging route step and swaying battle-flags, the remnants of that world-famous army; and remnants they were indeed. Regiments were so reduced in strength that they seemed not much larger than a color guard for the flags they carried, flags which they had borne to so many victories on so many hard-fought fields.

General Chamberlain, impressed with the momentous meaning of this occasion and filled with admiration for those passing men, gave a command. A bugle pealed. Never was an order so willingly executed. The long blue lines stiffened, straightened, and saluted, rendering the soldiers' mark of respect and recognition, from the Blue to the Gray.

General John B. Gordon, at the head of the Confederate column, straightened, turned, his voice rang out. The men marching between the Union lines heard it. They, in turn, shifted to "Carry Arms," the marching salute, the Gray in honor of the Blue. When the battleflags were placed on the ground, it was done lovingly but proudly while the Union troops watched, still at the salute, in awed silence.

The greater bitterness and misery that then spread through the land was not the result of the war years. It was the Reconstruction that followed the war, and the men responsible were the extreme radicals in Congress, thirsting for revenge against the South. They had no intention whatever of listening to the words of General Grant when he said, "Let us have peace."

President Abraham Lincoln was the only one who could have controlled them. If he had lived, the problems of Reconstruction would have been handled by different men. They would have been chosen from among those who had demonstrated that their feelings toward the South were similar to those shown by the soldiers of both sides toward each other at Appomattox. Men of good will from both North and South, working together, would have avoided the horrors of the Reconstruction period.

Index

Index

A

Adirondack (sloop), 73
Alabama (cruiser), 134
Albatross (gunboat), 74
Albemarle (ram), 123
Ames, Adelbert, 59–60, 63
Anderson, Aaron, 135
Anderson, Marion T., 43–45
Andersonville Prison, 68, 110
Andrews, James J., 86, 89
  executed, 87
Andrews Raid, 6, 84–94
  executions, 85
  purpose of, 86
Antietam, Battle of, 105, 124
Appomattox Court House, 12, 131
Arkansas (ram), 72
Armistead, Lewis A., 123
Aroostook (ship), 78, 80
Artillery warfare, 58–70
  World War I, 59
Atlanta, Battle of, 102
Australia (schooner), 32
Ayers, Richmond, 176

B

Baldwin, Frank D., 12–13
Baltimore *Evening Sun*, xvi
Banks, Nathaniel P., 50

Barnes, H., 158
Barr, Joseph F., xiv
Barrell, Charles L., 157–161
Beatty, Samuel, 44
Ben Hur (Wallace), 37
Bensinger, William, 85
Blair, Frank P., 112–114, 118–119
Blake, Robert, 134
Blockade runners, 83
B'nai B'rith, 18
Bowen, John S., 168–169
Box, Thomas J., 29
Bradley, Thomas W., 177–178, 179
Bravest Five Hundred of '61, The
  (Rodenbough), 33
Briscoe, Franklin D., 180
Brooklyn (ship), 10–11, 76–77
Brown, Wilson W., 89, 91–94
Browne, Junius Henri, 164
Buckley, John, 182
Buell, Don Carlos, 84–86, 90–91
Buffum, Robert, 85
Buford, John, 49
Bull Run, First Battle of, 14, 59–60
Bull Run, Second Battle of, 50, 97–
  99, 100, 105
Burns, James Madison, 27–29
Burns, W. W., 14
Burnside, Ambrose E., 145
Burrows, Julius C., 158
Butler, Benjamin F., 59, 136–143
  removed from command, 137
Butterfield, Daniel, 103–104

C

Caldwell, General, 179
Campbell, William, 89
  executed, 87
Cantor, Eddie, xiii
Carney, William H., 132–134
Carondelet (gunboat), 71–72
Cavalry warfare, 46–57
Chaffin's Farm, Negro troops at, 132–143
Chamberlain, Joshua L., 129–131, 182–183
Chancellorsville, Battle of, 20–21, 147–149, 172–179
  field artillery at, 60–62
Chantilly, Virginia, Battle of, 124
Charleston (steamer), 82
Charleston Prison, 19–20
Chase, John F., 60–62
Chicago *Daily News*, xvi
Chickamauga, Battle of, 95–96
Chickasaw (ironclad), 11
Chipman, Henry L., 158–161
Civil War
  beginning of, 4
  end of, 83
  opposition to, 144
  reasons for, 27
Clark, John Wesley, 156–157
Clem, Johnny, 95–96
Cody, William F., 10
Cohn, Abraham, 146–147
Colburn, A. D., 164
Congress (ship), 78
Cook, John H., 32–36
Coolidge, Calvin, xiii, xvi
Cooper, John, 10–11
Copp, Charles D., 23
Cranston, William W., 178

Crater, Battle of the, 132, 135–137, 147
Cumberland (ship), 78
Cunningham, Francis Marion, 18–19, 56–57
Cunningham, James S., 115
Cushing, Alonzo H., 123
Cushing, William B., 123
Custer, George Armstrong, 12, 57, 68
Custer, Thomas W., 12

D

Daring and Suffering (Pittenger), 85, 90, 93
Davis, Elmer I., 154–155
Davis, George E., 37–40
Davis, Joseph, 154–155
Davis, Theodore R., 112
Deane, John M., 40–43
Don (ship), 12
Donaldsville, Louisiana, Battle of, 50
Dorsey, Daniel A., 89
Dorsey, Decatur, 135–136
Draper, General, 142
Drummer boys, 95–110
Duncan, James K. L., 71
DuPont, Samuel F., 78
Durante, Jimmy, xiii
Dwight, William, 126

E

Earling, Elijah, 176
Early, Jubal A., 36–40, 53, 126, 154
Egan, William, 68
Ellis, A. Van Horne, 177
Ellsbury, George H., 45
Ellsworth, Thomas F., 22

Emma (schooner), 73

Ewing, Hugh, 118, 119, 164

F

F. B. Bruce (ship), 73

Fair Oaks, Virginia, Battle of, 150, 152

Farragut, David G., 74–75, 82, 135

Field artillery
  types of, 62–63
  See also Artillery warfare

Five Forks, Virginia, Battle of, 96

Fleetwood, Christian A., 139, 140

Foote, Andrew H., 71

Forbes, Edwin, 53, 128, 157

Ford, Henry, xiv, xvii

Fort Clark, 77

Fort Darling, 78–79

Fort Fisher, 1, 3, 137

Fort Gilmer, 138

Fort Harrison, 138

Fort Haskell, 41–43

Fort Hatteras, 77

Fort Jackson, 6

Fort McAllister, 119

Fort Mahone, 50

Fort Morgan, 83

Fort St. Philip, 6

Fort Stedman, 40–43

Fort Sumter, 4, 179

Fort Wagner, 132–134

Fortress Monroe, 78, 82

Franklin, Tennessee, Battle of, 20, 155

Fredericksburg, Battle of, xi, 23, 109, 147
  field artillery at, 65

Freedman's Bureau, 21

Fry, James B., 90

Fuller, William A., 87

G

Gaines' Mill, Virginia, Battle of, 102–103

Galena (ironclad), 76, 78–82

General (engine), 87, 88

Genesee (gunboat), 74

Geronimo, Chief, 21

Gettysburg, Battle of, 7, 82, 123–131, 155, 156, 172, 179
  casualties, 123

Gion, Joseph, 147–149

Gion, Mrs. Joseph, 148

Goldsbery, Andrew E., 116–118

Gordon, John B., 183

Grant, Lewis A., 20

Grant, Ulysses S., 36, 39, 111, 115, 116, 118, 119, 131, 137, 142, 145, 161–162, 164, 165, 169, 182, 183

Grant, Ulysses S., III, xvi, xvii

Gribeauval, Jean Baptiste de, 58

Griffin, Charles, 60

Groce, John H., 115, 118–119

Grubb, E. Burd, 173, 175

Gustavus II Adolphus, King, 58

H

Hale, O. B., 119, 121–122

Hammerstein, Oscar, xiii

Hampton, Wade, 65, 68

Hancock, Winfield S., 150, 179

Hanna, Marcus A., 31–32

Hardin, M. D., 126

Harper's Weekly, 41, 45, 112

Hart, Thomas, 177

Hartford (ship), 11, 74, 132, 135
Hartranft, John Frederick, 43
Haskin, Joseph Abel, 126
Hatch, John P., 125
Hawkins, Martin J., 89
Hawkins, Thomas, 135
Hawkins' Zouaves, 97
Haynes, Edwin M., 40
Hays, Will S., 95
Heintzelman, Samuel P., 60, 153
Heller, Henry, 178–179
"Hero, A" (Hale), 121–122
Hess, Carl, 99
Hickman, John, 75
Hills, William G., 51–54
Holland, Milton M., 139–143
Hooker, Joseph, 149, 179
Howard, Oliver O., 21
Howard University, 21
Hutchins, Stilson, xiv

I

Indian wars, 14
Infantrymen, 27–45
Isaac Smith (ship), 19
Itasca (ship), 11

J

Jackson, Frederick R., 23–25
Jackson, Thomas J. "Stonewall," 59, 103–104, 149
James Island assault, 25
Jews, 144–147
Johns, Henry T., 5
Johnston, Joseph E., 29, 143
Johnston, Willie, 96
Jones, Edwin S., 76

K

Kaler, James Otis, *see* Otis, James
Karpeles, Leopold, 145–146, 147
Kearny, Philip, 124, 150, 152
Kearsarge (ship), 132, 134.
Kennedy, John, 67–70
Kennedy, Paul, xvi
Kilpatrick, Judson, 141
Kineo (gunboat), 74
Knight, William, 89, 93
Kohen, Charlie, xi–xvii, 7, 17–18, 65–66, 91, 124, 126
Kohen, Mrs. Charlie, xv

L

Labille, Joseph S., 111–114
Lackawanna (ship), 11
Lafayette (gunboat), 71
Laman, Clarrisa, 94
Langbein, J. C. Julius, 97, 98
Lawson, John, 135
Lebroke, Corporal, 61, 64
Lee, Fitzhugh, 68
Lee, Robert E., 12, 86, 123, 124, 131, 137, 149, 154, 182
Lees Mills, Battle of, 96–97
Leonard, Patrick, 14
Leppien, George F., 61, 62
Leslie, Frank, 3, 25, 72, 157
Leutze, Emmanuel, 97
Libby Prison, 20, 24, 104, 141, 170–171
Lilley, John, 29–30
Lincoln, Abraham, xvi, 4, 9, 43, 78, 82, 84, 110, 136, 137, 143, 153, 179, 183

Little Big Horn, Battle of the, 12
Logan, John A., 119
Longfellow, Henry Wadsworth, 156
Longmode, A. J., 50
Longstreet, James, 50
Ludgate, William, 19
Lutes, Franklin W., 73
Lyle, Peter, 124, 125
Lyman, Joel H., 51–54

M

MacArthur, Arthur, 21–22
MacArthur, Douglas, 22
McBreen, Thomas, 176
McClellan, George B., 78, 82, 104
McClelland, James M., 116
McClelland, Matthew, 75
McGonagle, Wilson, 114–115
MacIntyre, John, 35
McIntyre and Heath, xiii
Mack, Alexander, 76–77
Mackie, John F., 77–83
McPheron, Wesley, xvii
Maines, George H., xiv
Manchester, William, xvi
Mansfield, Battle of, 32
Marblehead (gunboat), 134
Marion, Francis, 56
Martin, Edward S., 76
Mason, Elihu H., 85
Mattox Creek expedition, 12
Mayfield, John S., 18
Meade, George G., 26
Medal of Honor awards
  beginning of, 4
  brothers receiving, 96
  father and son receiving, 21–22
  first Negro receiving, 134
  number of, 10

only woman receiving, 9–10
twice awarded to same person, 10–
    14
youngest recipient of, 96
Merrimac (ironclad), 78, 80, 134
Merritt, Wesley, 65, 67
Michigan (gunboat), 73
Miles, Nelson A., 21
Missionary Ridge, Battle of, 21
Mississippi (ship), 74
Mitchel, Ormsby M., 84–87, 90, 91
Mitchell Raiding Party, *see* Andrews
    Raid
Mobile Bay, Battle of, 10–11, 76–77,
    83, 135
Monitor (ironclad), 78, 80, 134
Monongahela (ship), 74
Morrison, John G., 71–73
Mosby, John Singleton, 152–153, 157
Mulholland, St. Clair A., 61, 149–150
Mullen, Patrick, 12
Murphy, Anthony, 87
Murphy, Robinson B., 99–102

N

Napoleon I, 58–59, 145
Nashville, Battle of, 43–45
National Archives, 18
Naugatuck (ship), 78, 80
Naval warfare, 71–83
Neeley, James W., 148
Negro troops, 132–143
New Orleans, capture of, 6
New York *Herald*, 119
New York Times, The, xvi
New York *Tribune*, 170
New York *World*, 26
North Carolina (ship), 73

Quinlan, James, 14

O

O'Beirne, James Rowan, 151–152
Oliver, Thomas P., 182
O'Neil, Charles, 68
Orbansky, David, 147
Ossipee (ship), 11
Otis, James, xv, 1–4, 5, 7–9, 12, 18,
    65, 77, 127, 134, 144, 154

P

Packbauer, E., 75
Parke, John G., 51
Parrott, Jacob, 85
Pearson, Drew, xvi
Pease, Joachim, 134
Pelham, John, 63–65
Peninsular Campaign, 96–97
Penrose, W. H., 176
Pershing, John J., xiv, 31.
Peyser, Julius I., xiv
Philadelphia *Inquirer*, 149
Pickett, George E., 123
Piper, J. M., 180
Pittenger, William, 85, 90–91, 93
Pleasant Hill, Louisiana, Battle of,
    32–36
Port Hudson, 30–32, 50, 74–76
Port Royal (ship), 78, 80
Porter, David D., 123, 163
Porter, Fitz-John, 103
Porter, John R., 89
Post, Philip Sidney, 44
Purman, James J., 182

Q

Quay, Matthew S., xi, xii

R

Ranney, Myron H., 97–99
Reddick, William H., 85
Resaca, Georgia, Battle of, 29
Rhodes, Julian H., 50
Rhodes, Julius D., 47–51
Rice, James C., 130
Richardson, A. D., 164, 167
Richmond (ship), 11, 74–76
Ricketts, James Brewerton, 36–38
Robbins, Roland, xiii
Robinson, Samuel, 89
Rodenbough, T. H., 33
Rodgers, John, 78–80
Roosevelt, Franklin D., xv, 18, 126
Roosevelt, George W., 127, 128
Roosevelt, Theodore, 126
Rosecrans, William S., 90, 94
Rosenwald, Julius, xiv
Ross, Marion A., 89
Rush, John, 74–76

S

Sabine Cross Roads, Louisiana, Battle
    of, 32
Savage's Station, Virginia, Battle of,
    14, 104
Savannah (sloop), 77–78
Sayler's Creek, Battle of, 56–57
Schell, F. B., 117, 142
Schofield, John M., 20
Schubart, Martin, 147
Scott, John W., 89
Scott, Julian A., 96–97, 98
Seaman, Elisha B., 178
Sellers, Alfred J., 124–126

Seminole (steamer), 82–83

Seven Days' Battle, 82, 96, 103

Shadrack, Perry G., 89, 90

Shelton, W. H., 62

Sheridan, Philip H., 47, 57, 65, 68

Sherman, William Tecumseh, 26, 29, 112, 116, 119, 143, 161, 162

Shiloh, Battle of, 86, 95

Sibley, Charles, 173, 175–176

Sickles, Daniel E., 21

Sidman, George Dallas, 102–110

Sir William Peel (blockade runner), 83

Slavens, Samuel, 89

Smith, E. Kirby, 83

Smith, James, 89–91

Smith, John Justin, xvi

Smith, William F., 97, 141

Smithsonian Institution, xvi

Sowers, Michael, 54–56

Spanish-American War, xi, 21

Stahel, Julius H., 152–154

Stanton, Edwin M., 84, 94

Steele, Frederick, 119

Stockman, George H., 111, 113

Stockton's Independent Michigan Volunteers, 102

Stoddard, George, 99

Stones River, Tennessee, Battle of, 94

Stoughton, General, 153

Stout, Richard, 19–20

Stringham, Silas Horton, 77

Stuart, J. E. B., 46, 59, 63–65
    artillery of, 64–65

Surratt, Mary E., 110

Syracuse University, 18

т

Taylor, Forrester L., 173–176

Taylor, Richard, 33

Taylor, Walter H., 124

Ten Weeks with a Circus (Otis), 4

Tennessee (ram), 10–11

Tennyson, Alfred, 156, 165–166

Terry, Alfred H., 1, 143

Texas (engine), 87

Thirty Years' War, 58

Thompson, Allen, 96

Thompson, James, 96

Thompson, Thomas, 178

Thulstrup, Thure de, 120

Toby Tyler (Otis), 4

Townsend, E. D., 9

Trevilian Station, Battle of, 65–70

Trogden, Howell G., 118–122

Truman, Harry S, xvi, 18, 65–66

Turner, J. Thomas, 148

v

Van Vorhis, Nelson H., 139

Vantine, Joseph E., 75

Vaughan, Harry H., xvi, 66

Vicksburg, 111–122, 161–168

Virginia Military Institute, 28

w

Wainwright, Joel W., 175

Wainwright, John, xx, 1–4, 18

Walker, Mary, 10

Wallace, Lew, 36–40

Ward, William H., 161–171

Warren, Francis E., 30–31

Washington, George, 4

Washington *Post*, xiv

Waud, Alfred R., 55, 103, 151, 174

Webb, A. S., 129

Welles, Gideon, 82

Wheeling (W. Va.) *Intelligencer*, 15

Widick, Andrew J., 18
Wilderness, Battle of the, 145–147, 150, 174
Williston, Edward B., 65–67
Wilson, George D., 89, 90
Wilson, John A., 89
Wilson, Richard J., 173–175, 176
Wilson, Mrs. Woodrow, xiv
Winchester, Virginia, Battle of, 53–54
Winnebago (ironclad), 11
Wirz, Henry, 110
Wollam, John, 89
Wood, Mark, 89
Wood, Richard H., 114
Wood, Thomas J., 44

Woodbury, Eri D., 25
Woodruff, Carle A., 68
Worden, Jno. L., 78
World War I, xii, 10, 31, 66
    casualties, 59
World War II, 7, 21
Worthington, Glenn H., 39
Wright, Marcus J., 64, 117
Wright, Orville, xvii

z

Zook, General, 179
Zulu War, 110